YOU CAN

G000138859

Survive
your early years
OFSTED
inspection

Avril Harpley and
Ann Roberts

FOR AGES
3-5

"No warning, new grading…
the most dramatic changes
in years."
(*Nursery Education*)

Authors
Avril Harpley and Ann Roberts

Other contributions
Jean Evan: 'Introduction'; 'You Can...Prepare in different settings (1) and (2)'
Pauline Kenyon: 'You Can... Build a successful team'

Editor
Victoria Lee

Assistant Editor
Niamh O'Carroll

Illustrations
Mike Phillips

Series Designer
Joy Monkhouse

Designer
Andrea Lewis

Text © Avril Harpley and Ann Roberts
© 2006 Scholastic Ltd

Designed using Adobe InDesign

Published by Scholastic Ltd
Villiers House
Clarendon Avenue
Leamington Spa
Warwickshire CV32 5PR

www.scholastic.co.uk

Printed by Bell and Bain Ltd.
  2 3 4 5 6 7 8 9 6 7 8 9 0 1 2 3 4 5

Acknowledgements
Jean Evans for: 'Introduction'; 'You Can...Prepare in different settings (1) and (2)' © Jean Evans (2006, previously unpublished). **Pauline Kenyon** for: 'You Can... Build a successful team' © Pauline Kenyon (2006, previously unpublished).

British Library Cataloguing-in-Publication Data
A catalogue record for this book is available from the British Library.
ISBN 0-439-965-349
ISBN 978-0439-96534-7

Contents

Introduction **5**

Chapter 1 – You Can... Prepare positively. **7**
You Can... Meet Ofsted requirements (1) **7**
You Can... Meet Ofsted requirements (2) **8**
You Can... Identify everyone's roles **9**
You Can... Develop a positive approach **10**
You Can... Sustain a positive approach **11**
You Can... Build a successful team **12**
You Can... Overcome apprehension **13**
You Can... Prepare in different settings (1):
              childminding settings **14**
You Can... Prepare in different settings (2): crèches **15**

Chapter 2 – You Can... Self-evaluate successfully . . . **16**
You Can... Develop a schedule for self-evaluation **16**
You Can... Tackle Ofsted forms! **17**
You Can... Involve all staff **18**
You Can... Monitor the quality of provision (1):
              Every Child Matters **19**
You Can... Monitor the quality of provision (2):
              helping children to be healthy and stay safe . . . **20**
You Can... Monitor teaching and learning **21**
You Can... Monitor children's attainment and progress . . . **22**
You Can... Monitor management and leadership **23**
You Can... Identify strengths and areas for
              development **24**
You Can... Improve over time. **25**

Chapter 3 – You Can... Develop a long-term plan. . . **26**
You Can... Identify priorities **26**
You Can... Turn an area for development into a strength . . **27**
You Can... Develop a format for a plan (1): principles for . . .
              the format. **28**
You Can... Develop a format for a plan (2): layout and . . . . .
              content **29**
You Can... Build in resources **30**
You Can... Build in finances **31**
You Can... Set timescales **32**
You Can... Conduct annual reviews **33**
You Can... Make it a success! **34**
You Can... Involve staff and parents **35**

Contents

Chapter 4 – You Can... Plan a well-balanced curriculum
.... 36
You Can... Include the six Areas of Learning and the Early ...
Learning Goals 36
You Can... Include the Stepping Stones 37
You Can... Include the five strands (1) 38
You Can... Include the five strands (2) 39
You Can... Plan effectively (1): the right impact on the .....
children 40
You Can... Plan effectively (2): the issues of learning, staff ...
and management...................... 41
You Can... Address additional needs and inclusion 42
You Can... Balance adult-led and child-initiated activities . . 43
You Can... Meet the needs and interests of your children . . 44
You Can... Support professional development 45

Chapter 5 – You Can... Succeed with assessment and .
record-keeping 46
You Can... Build links with the curriculum 46
You Can... Construct a schedule..................... 47
You Can... Involve parents 48
You Can... Keep useful records...................... 49
You Can... Pass on the right information 50
You Can... Develop the Foundation Stage Profile 51

Chapter 6 – You Can... Build community links 52
You Can... Involve parents and carers with views and ......
feedback 52
You Can... Liaise with other agencies 53
You Can... Foster links with the local community 54

Photocopiables 55
Preparation for Ofsted starter checklist 55
Self-evaluations schedule support document 56
Observation and assessment of activities............... 57
Leadership and management questionnaire 58
Development plan 59
Identifying priorities and setting timescales............. 60
Annual review and professional development 61
Gathering evidence for the five key outcomes........... 62
Parents' and carers' questionnaire.................... 63

Introduction

Early years practitioners, especially registered childminders and day-care providers funded by the Government to offer nursery education to three- and four-year-olds, are constantly faced with new challenges. Since the late 1990's nurseries have regularly undergone two separate inspections, one by social services departments responsible for monitoring the care of the children, and the other by Ofsted, a non-ministerial government regulatory body responsible for monitoring the education of the children.

In the latter part of this period, the two inspections were combined so that inspectors became responsible for inspecting both the quality of care and education provided by a setting. Those responsible for care would give judgements based on 14 National Standards and those inspecting education would observe children's progress towards a set of Early Learning Goals within the Foundation Stage curriculum.

Ofsted inspections today

The inspection system introduced by Ofsted in April 2005 linked together the standards for care and nursery education under a set of outcomes (listed in *Every Child Matters*) that local authority children's services must work to deliver under the requirements of the Children Act 2004. Providers are now judged on how they help children to be healthy, stay safe, enjoy and achieve, and make a positive contribution. Early years providers must also consider how their organisation supports children's well-being. These inspections are unannounced.

How to use this book

With all of the above changes, it is understandable that many practitioners are apprehensive prior to an expected inspection. This book aims to allay these concerns and provide practical advice before, during and after the event.

For maximum benefit, initially, the whole of the book should be considered. The staff team should then prioritise those aspects of the inspection process that they feel they need most support with, using the activity page headings as the basis of a working programme. The book can also be used to 'dip into' when required.

The book can be used for reference along with the following useful publications: *National Standards for Under Eights Day Care and Childminding*, Department for Education and Skills, 2003; *Curriculum guidance for the foundation stage*, Qualifications and Curriculum Authority, 2000; *Every Child Matters*, Department for Education and Skills, 2003; *Early years: firm foundations*, Ofsted 2005; *Birth to Three Matters*, Department for Education and Skills, 2002.

How the book is organised
The overall structure
The book includes six chapters, each with a definite theme, and within each chapter there are activity pages focusing on different aspects of the theme. The book places great emphasis on the need to view the inspection process positively, and to develop a confident *I can do it* approach.

Chapter 1 sets the mood of the book, with suggestions for positive ways of preparing effectively for inspection. Chapter 2 is devoted to suggestions for monitoring and evaluating different aspects of provision, since the inspection process now includes a huge emphasis on self-evaluation. Chapter 3 explores ways of developing long-term strategies that will ensure continuous improvement of the setting over time. The inspection process evaluates a setting's contribution towards five key outcomes for children's well-being, and these are assessed against specific details set out in the document *Every Child Matters*. Chapter 4 therefore explains them in detail and discusses how to incorporate them in the overall organisation of the setting. The key outcome 'enjoying and achieving' is given additional focus. Chapter 5 provides suggestions to support practitioners in setting up, maintaining and monitoring their assessment and record keeping documents effectively. Chapter 6 provides helpful hints on forging strong links with parents, the local community and professional agencies.

The activity pages
Each chapter has a specific theme and this is subdivided into several activity pages, each focusing on a single aspect of that theme. The activity pages are structured as follows:
- A short introductory paragraph identifies the overall context for the activity page.
- General and legal requirements relating to the inspection process are listed for ease of reference.
- Short, thought provoking 'thinking points' are included to stimulate staff discussions and to draw attention to aspects that might easily be overlooked.
- 'Tips, ideas and activities' support practitioners with practical ways of making links between theory and their own practice.

The photocopiable pages
A selection of useful photocopiable materials in Chapter 7 link to specific activity pages, for example, to support planning or parent links. They can be used as they are and some can be enlarged according to requirements.

You Can... Meet Ofsted requirements (1)

Ofsted provides clear information concerning its requirements: what it looks for on inspection and how it makes judgements. You and your staff need to be fully conversant with the National Standards for Under Eights Day Care and Childminding, Every Child Matters *and, if applicable,* Birth to Three Matters *or* Curriculum guidance for the foundation stage. *There are four types of day care: full day care for under eights, sessional care that provides up to a maximum of four hours a day, crèches and out of school care. Early years advisers and the LEA are able to give advice to help providers prepare for an Ofsted inspection.*

Thinking points

1) Registration

● Ofsted requires settings to register with them.

● You must consent to Ofsted pursuing checks with a range of professionals. All adults working with children need a CRB disclosure – a criminal records check. Ofsted will supply the form DC2.

● Registration will set out staffing requirements.

● Your staffing records should include a contract for employment, details of wages, responsibilities and disciplinary procedures.

● You must inform Ofsted if there are any changes to the premises, the facilities or the provision; to personnel and their suitability, or any matters affecting the welfare of the children.

2) Inspection

● This is an on-site inspection.

3) Investigation

● Ofsted investigates any concerns about a setting.

4) Enforcement

● Ofsted will take action against a setting if there is any risk to the children.

General requirements

● Ofsted has four main functions: registration, inspection, investigation and enforcement.

Tips, ideas and activities

● Before applying to Ofsted for registration, make sure you meet its conditions and requirements. This includes confirming the suitability of any persons working or living in the setting, the premises, and the ability to meet the *National Standards* and curriculum requirements.

● Check on a regular basis that you have accurate records of staff qualifications and any relevant personal details.

● Make sure that the CRB police checks are up to date.

● Re-assess your staffing ratios and staff work patterns. Guidelines suggest that senior staff are qualified to NVQ Level 3 and at least 50 per cent of the rest of the staff to NVQ Level 2.

● Review contracts of employment, staff roles and responsibilities, as well as disciplinary and grievance procedures.

● Ensure that parents are aware of what to do if they have a concern or a complaint.

You Can... **Meet Ofsted requirements (2)**

In July 2001 the Government set out the Guidance to the National Standards for Day Care *showing what providers should aim to achieve and a set of regulations. They represent the minimum requirements for registered childcare providers. Recently a new set of outcomes was described in* Every Child Matters *that concern all children from birth to 18. In addition, there are two developmental guidelines for practitioners:* Birth to Three Matters *for the youngest children or, for those aged between three and four years, the* Curriculum guidance for the foundation stage.

Thinking points

● Inspections are made without any prior warning so it is essential that your paperwork is up to date. Inspectors will ask to see your completed self-evaluation form. The type of form will depend on your setting: SEF for the Foundation Stage and Key Stage 1, and *Are you ready for your inspection?* for early years.

● Inspectors will evaluate how well the setting is meeting the outcomes as described in *Every Child Matters*:

- staying healthy

- enjoying and achieving

- keeping safe

- contributing to the community.

- effective organisation.

● Check that you have all the relevant documents and that the staff have read them. Are there any gaps in your provision or documents that need to be completed?

● If you have had a previous inspection, make sure you have a copy of the last report available together with your action plan. Can you provide evidence that you have addressed any issues?

General requirements

● Inspectors will look at how well you meet the *National Standards*, taking into account *Every Child Matters* and either *Birth to Three Matters* or the *Curriculum guidance for the foundation stage.*

● Since April 2005 a new style early years inspection has integrated care and nursery education and therefore produces a single report under five headings.

Tips, ideas and activities

● Observe and question staff to assess how well they know, understand and apply the *Curriculum guidance for the foundation stage* (or *Birth to Three Matters*), *Every Child Matters* and the *National Standards for Day Care.* Check that all the staff have had ample opportunity to read and discuss all the necessary documents.

● Make sure all the relevant documentation and evidence is ready, available and accessible. Treat yourself to some attractive files to organise your paperwork and put aside time on a regular basis to keep filing up to date and organised.

● Invest in a camera so that you can record evidence of the children's work and play. Display and caption any photographs that link to the appropriate Standard or Early Learning Goal.

● Self-evaluation is the key to the new inspection framework. Make sure you have completed the form and have identified areas to address.

You Can... **Identify everyone's roles**

Being able to clearly identify everyone's roles and responsibilities within the setting will help you to be ready for an Ofsted inspection. A successful team is one where all the staff are deployed in such a way that their expertise is used to the best effect. Good leadership enables a group of individuals to pull together as a team, to share their skills for the benefit of the setting and to meet the legal requirements.

Thinking points

● The *National Standards* describe the roles required in a setting. In small settings this may mean that some team members have to take on responsibility for more than one area.

● Roles include the following: health and safety, fire safety, first aid, child protection, behaviour management, special educational needs and equal opportunity. You may also need a named person to support children who do not have English as their first language.

● Do you have procedures for appointing staff with specific skills, or clear criteria for allocating roles within the team?

● Make sure you have contingency plans for finding a replacement, should a named member of staff leave.

● Consult with team members to agree the key aspects of their role and accept responsibility for the tasks they are expected to perform.

● The identification of roles and responsibilities through a visual display is useful for informing staff, children and parents.

General requirements

● Inspectors will look for strong leadership in a setting where team roles are clearly defined and responsibilities are delegated appropriately.

● Staff records will be inspected. These should include details of qualifications, experience, training history and vetting procedures. Inspectors will meet staff to discuss their roles and examine policies, asking how these are implemented.

Tips, ideas and activities

● Review current roles so that they match requirements in the *National Standards*.

● Show photographs of all the staff with a description of their roles within the setting.

● Display key staff groups and staff rotas.

● Provide a bulletin board for information from subject or phase leaders or supervisors.

● Maintain staff records with contact details and training. Monitor areas where they may need further professional development.

● Supply files, appropriate software and relevant record-keeping resources for each named member of staff.

● Consult staff as to what they feel defines their role, and come to an agreement. It is essential that they are clear about the tasks, responsibilities, and the limits of their role.

● Make sure that staff are aware of the appropriate documentation and legislation. Cover the necessary areas at a staff meeting and follow up with accessible literature.

● Introduce a slot at staff meetings for named staff to feed back and inform colleagues or governors about issues that concern them.

You Can... Develop a positive approach

It is vitally important that the staff team who will undergo the inspection feel positive. There is a very fine balance between being positive and ready, and being overburdened and anxious. If staff are feeling positive, they approach an inspection with confidence and clarity. Providing high-quality care and education should be seen as an everyday occurrence. This approach has to come from the top. Staff who have positive leadership and support will have more energy and are able to cope better.

Thinking points

● To enable staff to feel positive, provide regular dialogue where opinions can be expressed and are listened to in a genuine and constructive environment.

● People's feelings and concerns may change over a period of time. Timetable regular staff meetings where staff can discuss possible questions that inspectors may ask and review any issues or worries.

● Make sure that staff feel valued for their work and acknowledge their contribution to the setting.

● What signals do staff receive to make them feel positive about the inspection process? It is important that all senior staff present a confident and united front. Think about how you can communicate a positive approach to all the staff.

● Knowledge is power: if staff understand the inspection process, they will feel less vulnerable and more positive. Provide opportunities for the staff to read the relevant documents and to raise any queries they might have on the procedure involved for inspection.

General requirements

● Inspectors take into account staff who demonstrate they have a positive impact on the children attending the setting.

● Encourage your staff to see the inspection as a constructive experience: someone from outside the setting can offer independent views and advice. The outcome of positive feedback is a clear development plan.

Tips, ideas and activities

● Get staff used to being observed by having observation days, but always have a debriefing afterwards – similar to Ofsted feedback. Ask staff what they thought they did well and why, and discuss this together.

● Make staff feel valued by planning rewards, such as an after-Ofsted meal for all the staff as a 'thank you'. This then paves the way for the development work needed afterwards, and it creates a positive springboard for the whole team.

● Ask staff to complete the statement, *I feel positive when...* This helps to formulate an idea of the conditions they need as an individual within a team to feel good. Positive emotions tend to be infectious – make sure these are not diminished by negative attitudes and responses.

● Encourage staff to think around, below and above problems – if staff begin to think laterally, they will feel nothing is impossible and that together they can manage anything. This positive outlook will make for a more supportive and constructive team.

You Can... Sustain a positive approach

Since inspections are unannounced, with no prior warning given, the idea that 'every day is an Ofsted day' needs to be firmly embedded in the mindset of all the staff. 'Be prepared always' has to be the mantra of every setting.

Thinking points

● Staff need to feel that their setting is a positive place to be and that they are valued members of a team. Any issues should be aired professionally and these need to be resolved quickly and appropriately. How is this currently achieved?

● Consider what the term 'sustainable' means and think of simple examples to illustrate this in your setting. Ask other staff to do the same.

● Encourage staff to develop, investigate and offer their own solutions to challenges facing them. They are more likely to feel positive about their role and responsibilities, and to be motivated to implement any new undertaking.

● If there appears to be a drop in staff morale, inject some enthusiasm – hold a social evening or provide a small reward.

● You will need to plan ahead to ensure that the positive approaches you put in place are sustained in the future.

General requirements

● Inspectors need to be convinced that the setting has a 'can do approach' to things. Attitude is important in the new format.

● Requirements, such as health and safety, must be maintained at all times. Make sure checks, rules and routines are in place for staff, children, paperwork and the setting environment, and encourage staff to be vigilant in implementing them.

Tips, ideas and activities

● Discuss short-, medium- and long-term plans with the staff. Ensure that they realise that every action has an effect on the whole setting. Write your plans on a large piece of paper presented like a mind map and display it for staff to see.

● Adapt the idea of the Stepping Stones and Early Learning Goals from the curriculum. A long-term plan can seem like a goal and the journey to that goal will have 'stepping stones'. Pinpoint some of the key achievements along the way – these will help to keep staff positive.

● Sustaining a positive approach means keeping up motivation levels. Staff may need to be given new ideas or be guided to think differently around issues. Initiate visits and training diaries to remind staff of what they learned and what they did as a result.

● Hold short briefings at the beginning or end of day; keep them short and end with a *thank you* or *well done* – always leave on a positive note.

● To have a positive approach, you need nourishment! Leave a fruit bowl or biscuits as a surprise when you sense things are slowing down in the staff area – with an appropriate message to all staff.

You Can... **Build a successful team**

One of the features of effective early years settings is strong teamwork. Teams may be large or small but should include all those people who contribute actively to your setting. All practitioners need to be team members – remember to also include staff such as welfare assistants, lunchtime supervisors and so on who may have a direct contact with the children in your setting. Here are some suggestions on how to create and sustain strong teams with a shared commitment.

Thinking points

● First identify all those people who constitute your team. You may have many 'layers' in your team, such as full- or part-time teaching and care staff, both regular (for example, welfare, lunchtime, caretaker, volunteers) and occasional (allocated support from other agencies, volunteers and parent helpers).

● Do part-time and occasional team members adopt the same approach to working alongside young children as full-time staff?

● How can you ensure everyone shares your setting's values – and knows what is expected of them? You need to develop ways to involve all staff, not just giving direction but getting feedback and suggestions from them too.

● Ensure that the whole team feel valued by inviting members to a schedule of specific (and convenient) meetings and social events.

General requirements

● Inspectors will want to know how well the group functions as a team, including how well all staff understand the policies and values of your setting, and how well they are able to demonstrate this in their approach with young children.

Tips, ideas and activities

● Display each team member's photograph on a public 'Our team' board.

● Invite everyone to help review the overall educational curriculum (once or twice a year), discussing forthcoming planning and how each team member can contribute.

● Hold 'bring and share' or 'takeaway suppers' (out of hours) to tackle practical issues and to share training – for example, the role of adults in child-initiated play.

● Arrange fixed meetings each term for involved staff to discuss term or half-term planning. Hold further weekly fixed meetings for detailed immediate planning and decision-making for those directly concerned, clarifying who does what, when, how and with which groups.

● If part-time staff members have difficulties attending, plan meetings at different days, times or venues to maximise attendance.

● Set up a 'Good communications' board, giving details of topics, arrangements and information for occasional visitors. Encourage everyone to use it.

● Have a team suggestions book for all to use – and refer to this at all meetings to value contributions.

● Produce a parents' and helpers' book which gives details of allocated activities, daily information and vital policies – to be read on arrival.

You Can... **Overcome apprehension**

It is normal to feel apprehensive about an inspection. When we are faced with a new or unfamiliar situation we usually go through a range of different feelings and reactions. Our first response is often negative, even shock. We may then have feelings of self-doubt and panic until we come to accept the situation and look for ways to respond. Finally we come through it and discover that we have grown because of the experience.

Thinking points
● Inspectors give judgements not opinions. These are based on the evidence you provide and what they see and hear.

● Try to be as organised as possible. Is your documentation, such as files, records, plans and data up to date and accessible?

● Remember that the inspector's comments and feedback are given to help you to improve your practice, not to distress you.

● Few settings achieve perfection – there are always areas that can be improved. Recognise this and learn from the inspection, in order to raise standards and quality.

● Know that feelings affect behaviour and your inner thoughts affect your feelings. Talk positively to yourself, inside your head, and take control. Do you ever allow your feelings to take control and you find that you have behaved in a manner you later regretted?

General requirements
● It is counter-productive to spend too much time discussing the negatives or complaining about them. Focus on the present rather than what 'might' happen. Make sure the inspection runs smoothly by being well prepared.

Tips, ideas and activities
● Think solutions, not problems.

● Write down how you feel about an inspection. Know that, when faced with a new situation, most of us will often exaggerate the outcome, generalise or make illogical assumptions, and have unrealistic expectations.

● Assess the situation and ask yourself, *What is the worst thing that could happen?* Be realistic: what is the probability of it happening? Explore this idea and see how with that outcome there could be advantages or opportunities.

● Put yourself in control by visualising yourself handling the situation. Use statements such as, *I can...* and, *I will... .*

● Make an achievable plan. See photocopiable page 55.

● Write a list of what needs to be done. Make it realistic and achievable, not dauntingly long. Ensure a task is displayed where all staff can see it and set deadlines. Use praise when each one is completed to foster a feeling of achievement and success.

● Talk with settings that have undergone an inspection. Concentrate on the positive benefits they got.

You Can... Prepare in different settings (1): childminding settings

Most practitioners facing an inspection find the prospect daunting. However, as childminders frequently work alone, they cannot share their anxieties about the inspection process with colleagues on a day-to-day basis, and may feel isolated and apprehensive. In order to be confident that the process of registration and inspection runs smoothly, childminders should understand what exactly is required of them. The relevant information can be found in the DfES publication National Standards for Under Eights Day Care and Childminding – Childminding *and the accompanying* Childminding: Guidance to the National Standards.

Thinking points

- Every childminder's situation is unique, so think about how you will help the inspector to form a clear picture of how you make maximum use of your home and the surrounding area to care for and educate children.

- Consider how you can collect evidence demonstrating how you maximise the advantages of home provision, for example, photographs of children helping to prepare meals and so on.

- Gather evidence to show how you have risen to the more challenging aspects of the requirements for childminders. Make a list – for example, you may have arranged a series of shared outings with other childminders so that children can enjoy peer-group activities.

- Choose attractive office equipment that does not look out of place in your home, yet provides secure storage for necessary documents.

General requirements

- All day-care providers, including childminders, must meet the *National Standards.*

- Childminders will have some indication of when the inspection is likely to take place. The inspector will ring beforehand to check whether there are any days in the coming week when it would not be suitable to visit. They are required to give at least two days notice.

Tips, ideas and activities

- When the inspector contacts you to arrange the inspection, try to re-organise your schedule, as far as possible, so that you can be available on the suggested days. Putting off the inevitable will lead to greater anxiety.

- Arranging a suitable time for feedback after the inspection can present problems to the childminder working alone. Have a few alternative possibilities so that you can arrange a mutually convenient time when the inspector rings.

- Try to examine areas used by the children through the eyes of an inspector. Could improvements be made to the environment?

- Avoid trying anything new to impress. The inspector would prefer to observe regular and familiar activities, a relaxed childminder and happy children!

- Have familiar activities available that you know the children can access easily, to give you time to speak to the inspector.

- Recognise that there is support available from the LEA, local childminding groups and childminding networks. The National Childminding Association of England and Wales website has further details: www.ncma.org.uk

You Can... Prepare in different settings (2): crèches

Crèches provide occasional care for children under eight for more than five days a year. If they run for more than two hours a day they need to undergo the registration and inspection process. The crèche groups may meet in permanent premises, such as shopping centres or sports facilities, or they may be established on a temporary basis, for example, at exhibitions or conferences.

Thinking points

● Consistency is the key to high quality care for children attending crèches, especially where there are lots of different staff. The inspector will check consistency while observing how procedures are put into practice. Are regular meetings held to ensure that all staff understand documentation and realise what is meant by 'maintaining a consistent approach'?

● Check that you can demonstrate that you provide learning opportunities to meet the needs of all the children. Compile a folder for each distinct age group detailing how play activities are organised to link with *Birth to Three Matters* and the Foundation Stage curriculum, and how they are extended for those who attend more regularly.

● Crèches sharing premises need to consider the impact of other users. Make sure you can explain to the inspector how you ensure children's safety. Can you identify potential hazards through risk assessments? Do you make a safety check before each session?

General requirements

● As registered care providers, those who organise crèches must meet the *National Standards*. The exact requirements can be found in the DfES publication *National Standards for Under Eights Day Care and Childminding – Crèches* and the accompanying *Crèches: Guidance to the National Standards*.

Tips, ideas and activities

● The inspector will ring to check whether there are any days in the coming week when it would be unsuitable to visit, and to ask for the times and ages of children attending. If there are several part-time staff and volunteers, check whether problems are likely to arise with the planned rota for the identified days the inspector may be calling; also ensure that adult numbers are sufficient to allow time to talk with the inspector without compromising provision for the children.

● Observe your room organisation from an inspector's viewpoint. Are different age groups cared for appropriately in separate bays?

● Check that your resources are sufficient to meet the needs of differing numbers of children and of varying ages at any one time. Could your system for storing and displaying resources be improved?

● In the absence of permanent display facilities, create portable display boards for children's work and any parent notices.

● Be ready to demonstrate that your partnership with parents is strong, despite the fact that children may stay for short periods and the group numbers may be constantly changing.

You Can... Develop a schedule for self-evaluation

Self-evaluation is an ongoing practice that every setting must adhere to. The self-evaluation schedule has to be clear and understood by all staff as the inspector may refer to it. The schedule can be in the form of a grid or checklist, using the outcomes for children as required in the document Every Child Matters *and in the Ofsted inspection paperwork (see your self-evaluation schedule in* Are you ready for your inspection? *– a support document that Ofsted sends to every registered setting).*

Thinking points

● The headings of the five inspection strands (health, safety, enjoying and achieving, positive contribution to the provision and local community, and organisation) may help staff to group things together more easily in a schedule. Talk about what evaluation criteria should be under which heading and why. Set a date to revisit your schedule and review it with the staff.

● The schedule needs to rate current practice, highlight actions and list evidence of successful completion. It also needs to highlight the impact on the children within the setting.

● Staff need to understand the word 'effective' – as this is a word used frequently in self-evaluation. What does this word mean to them? How do they know when things are effective?

● Look at your previous self-evaluation schedules or paperwork and adjust them to be compatible with the new Ofsted formats.

General requirements

● The self-evaluation schedule must be effective and up to date. The new format asks practitioners to grade themselves: grade 1 is outstanding and grade 4 is inadequate.

● Your schedule must cover: health, safety, learning, achieving and positive contributions to the community, and organisation. Other headings could include: quality of teaching; observations; organisation; training opportunities; partnership with parents and the community.

Tips, ideas and activities

● Take a single outcome, such as health, and look at the resources you have, for example: any schemes of work, books and events. Consider ways of developing these, and collect any evidence together in readiness for inspection.

● Invite visitors in, such as a local health visitor, a nutritionist or a health and safety expert. Ask them to observe your setting and give you feedback on how you can make improvements. Log these visits carefully. This will also show you are developing your setting to meet the needs of the children. Write these into your schedule and use them as supportive evidence.

● See photocopiable page 56 as an example of a schedule. You can use this as a basis of a template for your own schedule for self-evaluation.

● When you come to grade your setting, as part of the new self-evaluation format, be as honest and realistic as you can. There will, no doubt, be areas that your setting does excel in and others in which improvements need to be made.

● See page 47 for further advice on constructing a schedule.

You Can... **Tackle Ofsted forms!**

The revised inspection framework (April 2005) requires settings to complete a self-evaluation form. It asks the question, What is it like for a child here? *The form requires the provider to assess how well they meet the outcomes described in the document* Every Child Matters. *It consists of tick boxes, and providers grade their own provision on the same scale as the inspector, from a '1' for outstanding to a '4' for inadequate. A useful tick list for required documents is provided with the self-evaluation form.*

Thinking points

● Complete the form in good time rather than putting it off, and revisit it quarterly. Day care providers will normally receive no notice of the inspection. It is important, therefore, that all documents are kept up to date and reviewed regularly.

● Once you have completed the form, you will have identified areas that require attention. You need to show how you are taking action to improve. Self-evaluation is the key to the planning and review cycle. One of the inspection judgements is assessing the setting's ability to improve.

● When completing the form, it is useful to keep the *National Standards*, the *Curriculum guidance for the foundation stage* or *Birth to Three Matters*, and the Ofsted guidance *Are you ready for your inspection?* close by as reference.

● Have you evidence to show how you organise your childcare, promote the children's well-being and provide quality teaching and learning?

General requirements

● The self-evaluation form will be the starting point for discussion with inspectors. Think carefully about the grades and remember to add written comments on the form as to the reason for your grades.

● If you have not completed the form before the inspection, you will be asked to do it on the day.

Tips, ideas and activities

● Don't procrastinate. Say, *I want to complete this form* and not, *I have to.*

● Review your time management. Make an appointment with yourself to allocate time to research and complete the form.

● Be systematic in tackling the sections on the form; complete one at a time. Collect all the relevant information for each section. Start with the section you see as most difficult – once that is completed the rest should be easy.

● Equip your setting with attractive files, make them easily accessible and develop a filing system for each section of the form.

● Tape an index at the front, so you can retrieve and update information quickly. Colour-code the files into broad categories: records, assessment and regulations.

● Put 'inspection' on the staff-meeting agenda. Make sure all staff are familiar with the self-evaluation procedures and the way the inspection will be carried out. Enlist their help in collecting information.

You Can... Involve all staff

Asking all staff to contribute to the self-evaluation will help you be ready for an inspection whenever it arrives. A successful team is one where members at all levels are valued for their role and feel that they can contribute with confidence. By providing your own assessments you complement those of the external inspectors and help to build up a comprehensive picture of your setting. It can show how effectively you address the relevant outcomes from the document Every Child Matters, *and answer the question,* What is it like for a child here?

Thinking points

● Have you explained the purpose behind self-evaluation to all staff and agreed a focus?

● Be aware that some staff may experience a range of feelings and emotions towards self-evaluation. Some may feel anxious or confused, while others may feel angry or even resistant. Can you convince the staff that self-evaluation is not about fault-finding but about supporting them in order to improve the quality of the provision?

● Explain to your staff how the self-evaluation can make action planning more focused and more effective.

● Part of the self-evaluation process will require observations. This should be handled sensitively and may mean updating skills and training for staff.

● How can you build relationships with staff to create better understanding? Have one-to-one interviews to gain an idea of their expectations and perception of your setting.

General requirements

● Self-evaluation is specific to your setting, your staff, your children and the needs of your community. Self-evaluation asks *How well are we doing and how can we do better?* It is a continuing cycle for thinking and planning, implementing and doing, monitoring and evaluation, and learning and adapting.

Tips, ideas and activities

● Make sure that all the staff are involved and familiar with your self-evaluation policy.

● Have a well-prepared open discussion with staff in advance of the self-evaluation process, and explain what is required.

● Ask staff to reflect and consider their strengths and points for development. Then invite them to consider how the strengths can be shared and the points for development addressed.

● Let one member of staff evaluate another as they work with a small group of children.

● Ensure that all staff take criticism in a positive light. Use sensitive and diplomatic language in a professional, rather than personal, manner. Acknowledge strengths and skills where appropriate and remind staff that the aim of evaluation is to improve the overall quality of the setting.

● Ask the staff to look at one aspect of provision, for example, outdoor play. Encourage them to evaluate it together and ask how they would rate it in the setting's self-assessment.

You Can... **Monitor quality of provision (1): helping children to enjoy and achieve**

Helping children to 'enjoy and achieve' is the third outcome of Every Child Matters *and you must monitor the quality of your provision against clear guidelines on a regular basis. Standard 3 of the* National Standards for Day Care *is specifically linked to this outcome, so this should be your point of reference. The relevant guidance booklets for the* National Standards *are helpful and you should also use* Birth to Three Matters *or the* Curriculum guidance for the foundation stage, *taking into account its underlying principles as well as the Early Learning Goals and Stepping Stones for the six Areas of Learning.*

Thinking points

● The quality of your provision in helping children enjoy and achieve has to be sustained, but this can be difficult in times of sickness or staff turnover. Think of ways to address and overcome these sorts of problems.

● Include expectations and explanations of what 'quality' actually means in your setting in a member of staff's initial interview, their induction and any supervision sessions.

● Make sure you are able to present evidence of how you help children enjoy and achieve in your setting – how effective you are and how it impacts on the children.

● Prepare ahead and monitor your plans regularly in order to show the inspectors that you are keeping an eye on the quality of enjoying and achieving within the setting.

General requirements

● Inspectors need to see that the outcome is being met by all staff.

● They will look for indicators of quality, such as good presentation and well-understood policies that are implemented in the daily practices of the setting. They will observe how staff communicate, interact and support learning appropriately.

Tips, ideas and activities

● Discuss what makes a good quality activity. Look at the planning, presentation, communications, the children's responses and the learning outcomes. Are you able to relate the activity back to *Birth to Three Matters* or the *Curriculum guidance for the foundation stage*?

● Visit other settings to observe an activity. What areas do you need to develop individually or as a staff?

● In your own setting, observe how the staff engage with the children and how the children are stimulated through teaching and learning. What is the quality of interaction?

● Make sure that all staff set aside several times in the year when they can be observed by each other or by senior staff. The quality of children's teaching and learning provide the foundation for children to enjoy and achieve, so it is key to monitor provision on a regular basis. Becoming used to being observed also means that when the inspector calls it will be less daunting.

You Can... Monitor quality of provision (2): helping children to be healthy and stay safe

In order for children to be healthy they must be in a healthy environment. There must be a high standard of health and safety in all settings for the welfare of children and staff. Health and safety rules need to be followed every day; for example, basic levels of hygiene and cleaning are essential so that resources and play equipment are clean and safe. Outdoor areas need a daily check to ensure that nothing has been deposited in the area or damaged overnight. Staff must attend appropriate training to keep their health and safety awareness high.

Thinking points

● Keep clear records of any staff who hold first-aid certificates and check for expiry dates regularly. Ensure you have an accident book accessible to the inspector.

● Make sure you document and sign important health and safety routines to show that these have been carried out. This shows you are monitoring your actions and means that records can be referred to when necessary.

● Revisit accident procedures regularly. Are your accident sheets or books checked regularly to ensure dates and signatures are correct and filled in? The *National Standards for Day Care* set out health and safety requirements and these can be used as a checklist for your practice. If these requirements are followed and developed further then your standards will be deemed as satisfactory or above.

General requirements

● Inspectors are very aware of the importance of health and safety. Action will be taken, including possible cancellation of registration, should quality of care be found inadequate.

● Staff who prepare snacks need to know about food safety.

● Children must have access to drinking water at all times.

● Unsafe equipment should be removed or the area sealed off completely.

Tips ideas and activities

● Put time aside at a staff meeting to present and talk about different health and safety scenarios. Get all the staff involved in providing solutions to these and enable them to develop their responses to various issues that might arise in the workplace. This sort of discussion offers opportunities for staff to share their expertise and experience, and demonstrates the setting's commitment to tackling these sorts of issues.

● Display health and safety information on the staff noticeboard to raise awareness.

● Create simple check sheets for different areas of the setting, use them and see if standards do improve or health and safety awareness becomes greater.

● You must comply with health and safety at all times. The manager or leader of the setting has a duty to see that requirements are met. Outcome 1 (helping children to be healthy) and outcome 2 (stay safe) have immediate impacts on the children.

You Can... Monitor teaching and learning

Monitoring teaching and learning is integral to good practice and it has to be systematic and consistent. In the early years the aim is to show how well the children are progressing towards the Early Learning Goals. Monitoring must be built into planning and have a clear focus. It should be manageable and the information gained used to inform future planning. Good relationships are crucial too. When staff know their children well, they can plan the best way to develop their potential. The monitoring process has to be sensitive, supportive and constructive.

Thinking points

● By the end of the Foundation Stage children should have made good progress towards all the Early Learning Goals. Collect evidence of this progress from a range of sources, for example, the children's work and staff observations.

● You need to plan teaching observations carefully. Think about what you are looking for when monitoring teaching.

● When monitoring children's learning, focus on how the children respond to an activity, how they use the resources and what they produce.

● Check that teaching staff cater for the needs of all the children. Do staff encourage child-initiated activities and challenge the children? Are they proactive in responding to special educational needs, race and gender?

● Consider how staff manage children's behaviour, for example, resolving conflicts.

● Make sure that time and resources are used effectively. Do staff create create a broad and well-balanced curriculum across the six Areas of Learning.

General requirements

● All staff need to be fully conversant with the relevant early years documents. These documents describe attainment targets and progression for each stage of learning and development. Staff should use their professional judgement to determine children's progress.

Tips, ideas and activities

● Focus on 'one child a day'. Select a child in the group and ask all staff to contribute their observations, comments, and evidence of progress made by that child over an entire day. Build this into the timetable.

● Set up a specific task with a clearly stated learning objective. This may be an activity, an Area of Learning or a particular resource. Record children's interest and achievement. Use photocopiable page 57 to help you with this.

● Have regular scheduled discussions with staff about teaching issues or concerns. Discuss current methods of monitoring teaching and invite suggestions for improvements.

● Ask two practitioners to give an account of the same teaching activity. What can you learn about your setting's teaching practices from these two accounts?

● Make 'on the spot observations' of children's learning. Record these into children's portfolios.

● Observe how teaching is carried out in other settings to help you identify strengths and areas for development in your own setting.

You Can... Monitor children's attainment and progress

Monitoring is a continuous process of gathering information, evaluating and analysing it for improvements. Good practice means constantly questioning your setting in order to monitor children's attainment and progress effectively. There are four forms of assessment you should use: formative (throughout the year to enable you to check if learning is taking place, to pinpoint issues and, if necessary, take immediate remedial action); summative (towards the end of the year, summing up what has been achieved); diagnostic (when you need to analyse strengths and areas for development), and evaluative (to reflect on the effectiveness of the teaching and learning).

Thinking points

● Promote strong self-esteem among the children. It is important to focus on what children can do, celebrating their achievements and strengths rather than highlighting their failures.

● Assess the skills and training that staff need in order to carry out monitoring procedures. They need to be able to analyse data, reflect on it, develop practical solutions and communicate these effectively.

● Decide the specific reason for monitoring attainment and progress of the children. Is it to grade, to identify gaps in skills, or to inform future action? This will affect the method and the technique employed.

● Does your method of monitoring help you to recognise and define problems?

● Remember to review previous monitoring records and assess the effectiveness of subsequent action plans.

General requirements

● Your self-evaluation should enable you to produce an action plan, in order to improve children's attainment and progress. Such a plan will inform the inspectors of your setting's goals and it will also help you to identify individual children's learning differences.

Tips, ideas and activities

● The process for monitoring can be summed up in the words: 'Describe, discuss, decide and document' (from *Assessment in Early Childhood Settings: Learning Stories* by Margaret Carr, Paul Chapman Publishing).

● Devise simple and effective systems for storing your paperwork and documentation.

● Monitoring attainment and progress of the children produces a mountain of paperwork, so delegate responsibility wherever possible.

● Define, with all the staff, the characteristics of a good setting and use this as a benchmark to monitor attainment and progress of the children.

● Identify essential learning objectives to observe on a daily or weekly basis.

● Make sure you provide recorded evidence of levels of children's attainment and progress when reporting to inspectors, parents or carers.

● Regularly assess if you are delivering what you describe in your policies. Are these demonstrated in the attainment and progress of the children in your setting?

You Can... Monitor management and leadership

Management and leadership each require quite different skills. Management deals with organisation and administration and needs good analytical skills. A manager is responsible for the safe, efficient learning environment. Leadership is more to do with motivating, enabling, reflecting and self-evaluating. A leader inspires, empowers others, listens, supports, and clarifies the vision and objectives. A leader needs good communication skills, secure values and beliefs. Every member of the team should feel valued and know that they are making a significant contribution to the setting via good leadership and management.

Thinking points

● Self-evaluation involves analysing the progress made towards an objective and helps to define what else has to be done.

● Ask yourself if your aims are reflected in your practice. Do policies stand up to scrutiny and are staff clear about their roles and responsibilities?

● Consider how and when you consult and inform parents or carers of their children's progress.

● Do all staff have regular annual appraisals?

● Can you show that the setting has a clear structure, with aims and values that are understood and implemented by all staff?

● Can you provide evidence that the children are making progress towards the Early Learning Goals and the Foundation Stage?

● Do you have evidence to show you monitor teaching and learning and use the evaluations to improve practice?

General requirements

● Inspectors will make four judgements regarding the effectiveness of the leadership and management. They will talk to parents or carers, staff and children, and examine documentation.

● Inspectors require evidence that the setting is committed to improving care and education for all its children. Make sure you can provide this.

Tips, ideas and activities

● Ask an external adviser to observe and comment on your setting's leadership and management.

● Investigate the possibility of joining an accredited Quality Assurance Scheme.

● Ask team members to complete an anonymous questionnaire to investigate what it is like to work in the setting. (Use the photocopiable on page 58 to help.)

● Encourage an atmosphere of mutual trust among staff. Observe each other's classroom practice and share constructive feedback. Use a consistent observation sheet.

● Have a 'Suggestion box' so that staff may submit items for the agenda at staff meetings.

● 'Share the chair': rotate the roles at staff meetings to encourage staff involvement and personal development.

● Implement annual staff appraisals.

● Tailor staff training and development opportunities to personal needs of staff and also the needs of the whole setting.

You Can... Identify strengths and areas for development

Identifying strengths and areas for development is a very useful exercise from which to plan the future progress for your setting. It is a good idea to ask a mentor or adviser from your local authority to observe your setting for these strengths and areas for development, as you may not recognise all of these by yourself. Prepare evidence to support what your setting's strengths are and have an action plan ready to address areas that need to be improved.

Thinking points

● The action plan is a working document, so keep it up to date and add in your evidence to prove when an area for development has been improved.

● How can you demonstrate your setting's strengths and how can you prove that these are effective?

● Areas for development change over time so date all paperwork and revisit your documents to review progress.

● Start by thinking of about three strengths and three areas for development in the setting. What criteria have you used to identify these?

● Do all your staff agree with your identification of these strengths and areas for development? Come to a consensus so that the team can work together on the targets ahead.

General requirements

● It is essential to demonstrate to the inspector that any areas for development identified in the last inspection have been addressed.

● Draw up an action plan ready to show the inspector. This should identify what needs improving, how it will be improved, who will do it, where and when it will be achieved.

Tips, ideas and activities

● When tackling an area for development, use the philosophy of stepping stones, for example: set the goal and plan the stepping stones that will enable you to achieve it.

● Choose one person as a monitor to check if things are being done and another as an evaluator to look at how well they have been achieved. This will help you improve the areas for development consistently.

● Solely concentrating on areas for development can mean becoming complacent with strengths. Consider how you can move further with your strengths and ensure they are sustainable. It is important not to let the current standards of your strengths slip.

● Organise regular meetings to discuss strengths only, so that the setting does not forget about them and their maintenance.

● See also 'You Can... Turn an area for development into a strength' on page 27 for more information.

You Can... **Improve over time**

Some improvements need to be immediate and prioritised, especially if the situation is in any way detrimental to the well-being of the children or staff. All improvements need to be embedded into an overall long-term plan for your setting. Checking against this plan is paramount, otherwise making progress may be forgotten in the busy day-to-day running of the setting. When looking at the spectrum of time allocated for improvements, set aside a month for short-term, three months for medium-term and six months for long-term improvements.

Thinking points

● Do you have any evidence of improvements for the inspectors to see? Keep a log, diary or scrapbook of the processes you have planned and show clear examples of progress being achieved.

● Review the setting's improvements on a regular basis. Set yourself reminders (on your calendar or computer, on a Post-it Note or in your diary).

● Put time aside to discuss and check with staff any improvements being made. It is important that staff are both consulted and notified so they are not left 'out of the loop'.

● Bear in mind that inspectors will talk to staff in order to make judgements on how effective they are at addressing the outcomes for children (see Chapter 4 for more information on this).

General requirements

● Inspectors will look at how well improvement is being managed. They need to be convinced that steps for improvement are taking place.

● They are more likely to accept that improvements are taking place if there is evidence of a clear action plan that factors in specific time limits, along with examples of progress.

Tips, ideas activities

● Hold success parties: when a goal for improvement is completed, celebrate it with a staffroom party or gathering. If extra work has been involved, remember to acknowledge this. At the same time, do not forget to note some type of evidence for the improvement to show the inspectors.

● Display a timeline on a wall either in the staffroom or on a board. Include any relevant 'milestones' on it and, when you reach a particular milestone, collect evidence of the quality of the improvement.

● Conduct a monthly review with the staff. Ask questions such as: *What have we achieved in this month? What do we need to achieve next month?*

● Make sure all staff are involved and informed of improvements being made. Staff need to feel that 'things are getting better' to maintain a positive attitude. Also it is through the staff that any changes will generally be implemented.

You Can... **Identify priorities**

Having a long-term vision and sharing it with the team in your setting is very important. You will need to manage and assess your plan in terms of priorities. The ability to prioritise is an essential skill of management and leadership, and you will need to make logical decisions based on good information and taking into account the outcomes described in Every Child Matters.

Thinking points

● Does everyone in your team agree on what the term 'priority' means? Your staff may have different ideas as to what constitutes a priority in your setting. Take time to discuss this together and to try to reach a consensus.

● With your staff, collectively define what you see as long-, medium- and short-term priorities for your setting.

● Once a priority has been identified, it is important to know the reasons for the decision. Make sure all the staff have a clear understanding why this issue was chosen to be a priority.

● Have you conducted a self-imposed check and decided on the areas you need to develop? The inspector will want to know that the management of the setting is effective and efficient.

General requirements

● The health, safety and protection of the children in your setting are paramount. The inspector will want to be assured that, when prioritising, the children remain the focus.

● The inspector will look for effective leadership and management in the implementation of the setting's aims and objectives.

Tips, ideas and activities

● Select three areas that are considered priorities. Write them on a large card and present them to your team at a staff meeting. Ask staff to consider and discuss each of these in turn. Focus on the impact they would have if completed, for example, the effect on the children, the staff and the setting. Decide which area has the most value and then put the three into a priority order.

● Take three key areas that may not be immediately possible to achieve, (they may include finance or training, for instance) and work through these together. Discuss with staff the reasons why one area may be more important than the others and finally put them in priority order. This exercise will assist staff in having a wider perspective and approach on how to prioritise areas more systematically. Write these on a timeline and then decide how to manage them so that they are achieved.

● Ask staff, parents and children what they consider as a priority for your setting. Compare and contrast their ideas. Is there one area that appears important to all?

You Can... Turn an area for development into a strength

Every setting has areas that they can improve and develop. Education is fast-changing, and change involves evaluating where you are and where you need to be. Identifying an area for development is a real skill and needs to be handled with sensitivity. Bear in mind that it can be an uncomfortable process for those concerned. Moving forward means celebrating and acknowledging strengths, but also transforming areas for development into strengths through professional growth.

Thinking points

● Do your staff all agree on the setting's strengths and areas for development? Organise discussions with your staff to find out. These discussions should be non-threatening and allow honest and open communication.

● Do not use the terminology of 'weaknesses' in your discussions with staff as this has negative connotations. The term 'areas for development' encourages a much more positive approach and attitude.

● Are your staff receptive to criticism? Colleagues find it hard to be critical of each other, but point out that positive criticism is essential in order to improve.

● How do you know if an issue is an area for development? Decide what the evidence is telling you. List these points and discuss them with staff.

● Is the criteria that you currently set to identify areas for development appropriate? Does this criteria need changing or updating?

General requirements

● Inspectors will want to see that your setting is using self-evaluation and acting upon it.

● Once an issue has been identified as an area for development, your setting needs to show how you will address it. It is vital to gather evidence to show development and progress.

Tips, ideas and activities

● Request support and advice from relevant early years advisers or consultants in order to address particular areas for development. Key staff might need to undertake further training or the setting may decide to involve the whole staff in order to change current practice.

● Ask staff to individually write down things that are currently positive and negative practice. Compare their ideas: is there a common theme?

● Identify one area of development that needs to be improved in your setting. What evidence do you have to prove to the governors, parents and, most importantly, the inspectors that it is changing and developing for the better?

● Set up two display boards: one for celebrations – looking at what you have done well – and the other, a focus board, which is centred on improving an area for development. Take down the celebrations board after one month and start to fill it with the outcomes or progress so far of the work you are doing around the area for development. This is the beginning of monitoring the changes and improvements.

You Can... **Develop a format for a plan (1): principles for the format**

Having a plan helps those working in the setting to have a focus and directs their energies towards given goals. To external visitors a plan summarises the objectives of the setting. However plans must be evaluated and followed or else they have little value. For a plan to be effective, it must also be presented in an appropriate format for those who will be following it. It also needs to take into account the outcomes in Every Child Matters.

Thinking points

● What does 'long-term' mean for your setting? Discuss this together with all the staff.

● Write the dates for goals to be achieved in your plan so that all the staff (and the inspectors) can see the time frame.

● Check that your long-term plan is succinct. Avoid unnecessary detail, but keep to the point on all issues.

● Link self-evaluation into your long-term plan. Make sure your plan includes forms of self-evaluation as this is a key element of the inspection process; for example, evaluating the health and safety of your setting.

● Communicate your setting's long-term plans to parents and carers. How can you communicate these plans in a positive way to them? Inspectors will be looking out for evidence of this.

General requirements

● A long-term plan should identify developments and improvements – inspectors will need to see that these are realistic and well-paced. Long-term planning must also include elements of sustainability and upholding standards.

● Any outstanding items from the previous inspection should be addressed through the long-term plan as well as any new items.

Tips, ideas and activities

● Ask someone from outside your setting, for example, your local early years adviser to look at your long-term plan and advise you on how you can improve it. Can they recommend or organise some training to help you?

● Include timelines for different goals in the plan – but make sure they do not all start at once. Stagger them so that you can concentrate on one at a time, giving each your full attention.

● If you know that limited finances or other factors will impact on your ability to achieve a certain target, make sure this is outlined in the long-term plan, so that inspectors are aware that, while you have understood and addressed the areas for development, you are waiting for improvements in funding, for example, to help you achieve the target.

● Look for ways of keeping parents and carers up to date with your long-term plans for the setting, without going into too much unnecessary detail – for example, pin regular notices on a noticeboard.

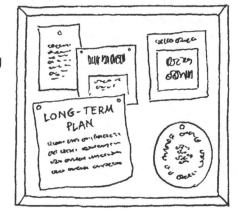

You Can... Develop a format for a plan (2): layout and content

A long-term plan is best set out in a grid format, as staff (and inspectors) have little time to read pages and pages of detailed text. The areas for development need to be placed in the first column and the methodology, timing, monitoring, finance and success criteria need to follow. Use photocopiable page 59 for your long-term plan or, alternatively, you may wish to adapt it to suit your needs. Some settings have one common format for all staff and then separate formats linked to specific areas or teams.

Thinking points

● Consider how you should present your plan. You may wish to write it by hand or present it electronically on the computer. Remember that an electronic plan can be updated and added to much more easily than a handwritten version.

● Make sure that your long-term plan is user-friendly. You need to include all the information in a way that is uncomplicated and easy to understand.

● If you are producing the plan on a computer, you can make the document look attractive and easier to comprehend by using different type sizes, colours and so on. However, do not over-design your plan, as this will make it harder to read.

● Check that your long-term plan includes whole-setting targets and other specific room, area or team targets, for example: improve outdoor play for all ages.

General requirements

● Remember that Ofsted is a regulatory, not an advisory body, so inspectors will not tell you how to lay out a plan. However, a well-presented plan with correct terminology and acknowledgments of requirements will demonstrate that you are aiming to improve your setting as a whole.

Tips ideas and activities

● Visit other settings and ask them about the format of their plans.

● If you identify another setting with similar areas for improvement, then you could work together for advice, feedback and support regarding your long-term plan.

● List the kinds of methodology the staff need to use in order to achieve the goals in the long-term plan. This might include, for example: on-site visits, visits to other sites, staff meetings, using reference books and internet research, fundraising, speaking to parents and carers, sending out questionnaires and conducting observations.

● In the monitoring column you need to state how and when you intend to monitor a particular area of development. You must also state who is being monitored.

● Under the finance column in the plan you should cost out all the areas you need to develop. Remember some goals may be set to be achieved in six months time, or longer, so add in extras for price increases. If staff are attending courses, budget these in to cover costs.

● Under the section for success criteria you must produce measurable evidence to show an area is in fact becoming successful in reaching its goals.

You Can... **Build in resources**

Settings need to operate on a cost-effective basis. It is important to look at resources as part of a long-term plan for your individual site. Resources include: staffing, sundries, equipment, repairs, emergency costs and various miscellaneous items. An Ofsted inspector is a regulator and so cannot as an individual advise specific resources that you should buy or have. Inspectors will be looking for a compliance with National Standards – so it is important to re-read the standards on equipment and resources, and be confident that the resources you have meet those standards.

Thinking points

● Consider the accessibility and range of toys and learning materials in your setting. Are they good enough quality? Do you need more of any particular type of item to meet the needs of all the children?

● Look carefully at the children's eating areas for lunch or snack times. They need to be clean and well-maintained at all times.

● Make sure that the resources you wish to invest in are essential to the development and improvement of your setting.

● Be realistic in your long-term planning. Ensure you include some leeway for price increases and salary rises.

● Think about ways to identify assistance to help you achieve investment in future resources, for example, the early years and childcare partnership or the lottery fund.

General requirements

● Inspectors will check that the children's intellectual, social, emotional, spiritual, physical and sensory development are reflected in your range of resources, and whether they are considered in your future plans.

● There needs to be a sufficient quantity and quality of resources to ensure comfortable play and learning, and health and safety.

Tips, ideas and activities

● Compile a wish list of items that the setting would like in the near future, asking your staff for their input. List each item in order of priority of need and attach some costings to each item. Use an up-to-date catalogue to price them.

● It can be useful to review toys and equipment in relevant magazines or test resources from suppliers. Acting as a tester can often result in the setting being sent free resources.

● Some courses run by the early years and childcare partnership support settings by including some appropriate resources. If this is already in your action plan, then this will help you to meet the objectives quicker.

● Show the inspector your long-term plan, especially if this indicates that you have identified areas for improvements and that additions to resources will be made in six to 12 months time. The long-term plan gives evidence of your vision for the setting and the development of its resources.

You Can... **Build in finances**

Provision for early years is varied as some settings are linked to schools, some are independent and others are private businesses. This means that the issue of finance is quite individual and site specific. Unfortunately finances can dominate and hinder progress at times. However, having good knowledge of the local community, charities, parents and their employment can sometimes assist, since asking for information or inviting in helpers can save cash.

Thinking points

- Good financial housekeeping makes sense in order to make the greatest impact on the setting.

- Plan ahead for all necessary expenditure, so that you know what finances you need to put aside.

- Consider all potential sources of finance for your setting – are there any unexplored areas of funding, for example: local community projects, the lottery or early years grants from your local authority? Sometimes you do not know what is available until you start to look.

- Think about how you make and save money for the setting, for example: hold some fund-raising events or ask parents to have a spring-clean and see if they could donate any appropriate, unused toys or equipment. (These would need to be thoroughly cleaned and checked for safety.) Are there materials you could recycle?

General requirements

- You must include financial housekeeping in your long-term plan so inspectors can see you are aware of your resources. Ofsted inspectors are not financial auditors, however finance is relevant to the outcome 'organisation' and they will want to know how effectively resources are being used, and the subsequent benefits to the children.

Tips, ideas activities

- In your long-term plan, bear in mind times like the end of the financial year when trying to push orders through can be difficult. Always plan in some contingency finances, as having some emergency funding will help reduce stress and worry.

- Have a complete audit of your cupboards. Put aside a day where unused items are all brought to one place. Let all the staff look over these and ensure they are not ordered again.

- Ask for suggestions and ideas from other organisations on how to make savings and to make your setting cost effective. National organisations such as the National Day Nurseries Association in the past has run courses on nursery finances, and Learning Direct runs courses that could give senior staff more business skills.

- Make sure all your staff understand the importance of finance and the impact that it can have on the effectiveness of your setting. For example, highlight issues such as unnecessary telephone calls and wastage from lights being left on and so on.

You Can... Set timescales

Effective planning requires careful thought and preparation and it is, therefore, essential that you allocate sufficient time for the process. A long-term plan defines your aims and principles. It sets the ethos and atmosphere of the setting, stating clearly why you do what you do, and where you want to be. All staff working in a setting should be aware of, and committed to, the aims, principles and the timescale of the plan.

Thinking points

● Curriculum-planning is a continuous process and divided into three parts: long-term, medium-term and short-term goals. The long-term curriculum plan identifies broad objectives by the end of the Foundation Stage. The Foundation Stage curriculum covers a two-year period and provides details of developmental Stepping Stones towards the Early Learning Goals.

● Timescales also need to be thought out for your setting for other long-term planning issues, such as developing quality provision and standards.

● There are a number of stages to go through before the long-term plan is written:

- identify strengths and areas for development, using the self-evaluation form to decide priorities

- develop solutions, asking named staff to be responsible for any action, using a timescale

- set objectives, writing statements of what you hope to achieve and by when.

General requirements

● Long-term plans take into consideration the curriculum, staff professional development, human and physical resources, expansion and any long-term work, such as building or renovation. The actual timescales to achieve the targets within your plan should be discussed with staff, governors or the committee and prepared well in advance so that they can be put in place for the coming year.

Tips, ideas and activities

● Schedule regular staff meetings to focus on long-term planning and to set timescales.

● Refer to the documents *Curriculum guidance for the foundation stage* or *Birth to Three Matters* to help you focus on the ethos and aims of your setting.

● Invite feedback from staff about previous timescales for achieving targets. Were these timescales realistic and successful? This will help you set better timescales in the future.

● Use photocopiable page 60 to assess which issues are urgent. This will help you decide priorities and define timescales for action.

● Create a timeline showing when objectives need to be completed and display this on the staff noticeboard.

● Celebrate achievements and successes for completing a target on time. Thank and reward staff for their cooperation and effort.

● Remember that timescales are not always set in stone. Sometimes they need to be flexible in order to take into account the unexpected.

You Can... **Conduct annual reviews**

Annual reviews are essential for an effective long-term plan for your setting. An annual review with individual members of your staff provides a chance to summarise past performance and establish new goals through a formal and open two-way conversation. It helps to establish the standards of performance and competencies required for the job, and it is also a forum for career development. On occasions it may provide evidence for extra responsibilities or a salary increase. Annual reviews are a powerful tool in the promotion of staff development.

Thinking points

● Are you a good listener when conducting a review? Take time to improve any skills needed for the review process.

● Ask staff to estimate their own progress towards each target. Encourage self-criticism. Staff are more ready to accept criticism when they have already recognised their own strengths and areas for development.

● Concentrate on performance not personality.

● If there has been a problem, try to describe the facts in a friendly manner, be specific and make sure you have evidence to support your comments. Develop a joint plan, looking for solutions together. Motivation to succeed is stronger if you use their ideas.

● How do you record or log these annual reviews? It is good to have evidence for the inspector.

General requirements

● Although annual reviews are not a legal requirement, they demonstrate good practice and long-term planning through self-evaluation procedures.

● It is the setting's responsibility to maintain the suitability of the staff and ensure that training, certificates and qualifications are kept up to date.

Tips, ideas and activities

● The annual review session should be carefully structured. Staff need time before the meeting to reflect on their past performance and to think about their future training needs.

● Each job has specific skills and competencies. Have the relevant job description at hand, as this will help you review past performance and set agreed targets. Good targets are specific, manageable, achievable, realistic and time-based.

● Practise assertiveness skills with a close friend or colleague. These will help you state facts, feelings and requirements during annual reviews with your staff.

● Prepare a checklist of skills and competencies required for each job. See photocopiable page 61.

● Make sure the annual review takes place in a private space with no interruptions. Provide simple refreshments. Make sure you have all the evidence you need for the meeting.

● Give each member of staff an agenda prior to the meeting so they can prepare for it. Make sure staff know the reasons and purpose of a review meeting.

● Give thanks and praise for progress alongside constructive feedback.

● Set a follow-up date, and keep records up to date.

You Can... **Make it a success!**

Once a plan is written, it requires focus and constant reference to make it a success. An important aspect of leadership and management is to sustain motivation while reviewing progress and making adjustments. This happens best when there is a regular open exchange of information. All staff need to be aware of their part in the long-term plan, what is expected of them and how they will be supported.

Thinking points

● Make sure that all staff are clear about their responsibilities. Do they know what needs to be done and do they have the necessary resources? Are they given reasonable time to complete a target? Do they know who to turn to for advice and support?

● Delegate responsibility and find the best person for a task.

● Check how much autonomy you give to staff when it comes to achieving targets. Can they make decisions, approve spending and access training?

● Ensure you provide regular time slots in the staff meeting agenda to address planning. Invite relevant staff to feedback on their progress.

● Consider how you assess success. Are there areas in the plan that need to be adjusted or revised? Certain targets take time to show their impact. Keep a record of progress so far and if necessary build into next year's planning.

General requirements

● A long-term development plan should be manageable with possibly only four or five main priorities. These should be realistic and achievable.

● The targets should be clear with specific criteria to measure success.

● Review the plan at regular intervals to ensure you are carrying out the relevant actions, or to make adjustments.

Tips, ideas and activities

● Improve the effectiveness of your plan by breaking down targets into small stages. This helps because you do not have to try to achieve everything in one go.

● Make your plan a working document. Highlight points and add comments along the way. Date and sign targets when completed.

● Vary the way you communicate your plan. Use face-to-face discussion, written memos, visual posters, notices on the board, small-group dialogue and formal and informal meetings.

● Display planning openly, so that everyone involved knows what is happening. Make an interesting visual display of 'progress so far'.

● Consider the work/life balance and staff workload. If you give them extra responsibilities, take the pressure off elsewhere.

● Celebrate success together! When a target on the long-term plan has been achieved, take time to thank staff and to recognise their contribution. Also remember to share progress with the parents.

You Can... **Involve staff and parents**

Inspectors will want to know what steps you are taking to accommodate parents' views and their differing needs when developing a long-term plan. Parents are your clients and they should be kept regularly informed about their children's progress. Constant communication and feedback from parents is an important aspect of the planning process. It also helps to build links between the child's two environments of home and the setting, and makes staff much clearer about what is expected from them. In order to create a happy and relaxed atmosphere, staff members and parents need to feel their input is worthwhile.

Thinking points

Staff

● Provide a good induction programme for staff so they understand the ethos and expectations of the setting.

● Check staff are fully aware of the policies of the setting and realise how these are implemented.

● Ensure that staff know the procedure for making their opinions and comments heard.

Parents

● When liaising with parents, be aware that some may feel hesitant while others may be demanding, even aggressive.

● Make sure you know what the parents' expectations are, both for their child and of the setting.

● Consider how often you meet parents. Are these occasions formal or informal? What is the focus of the meetings?

● Check if all parents have access to the Foundation Stage curriculum and the Early Learning Goals.

General requirements

● Staff must be able to engage with parents and report to them positively about children's achievements. Standard 12 requires inspectors to look for evidence showing how you share children's progress with parents.

● Staff need attentive listening skills to respond to parents' concerns.

● Feedback should be incorporated into the development of the setting.

Tips, ideas and activities

● Develop a mentoring scheme for staff, so that they have a more experienced member of staff to go to for advice and support, if necessary.

● Plan events where you meet staff and parents for both information and pleasure, for example: hold informal sessions where parents can join their children, coffee mornings so that parents can meet each other, fund-raising events, curriculum workshops, special social events for staff in order to enhance team spirit and so on.

● Create an attractive area within the setting where parents feel welcome and comfortable and able to talk in private.

● Employ a variety of techniques to share information with staff and parents, including written, oral, visual and interactive. You could, for example, use photographs or presentations to promote discussion about activities and the curriculum.

● Arrange flexible appointments to fit in with staff and parental work patterns.

● Review your plans for involving parents and staff on a regular basis and ask for feedback on how you are doing.

You Can... Include the six Areas of Learning and the Early Learning Goals

A broad and balanced curriculum is the right of every child in the Foundation Stage. It is the responsibility of the practitioners to take note of the Early Learning Goals and organise activities around these while also meeting the children's individual needs. It is vital that the structure of the Foundation Stage curriculum is known and understood.

Thinking points

● There are six Areas of Learning in the Foundation Stage curriculum and there are clusters of Early Learning Goals for each Area. The Areas of Learning are:

● Personal, social and emotional development

● Communication, language and literacy

● Mathematical development

● Knowledge and understanding of the world

● Physical development

● Creative development.

● The Foundation Stage is aimed at three- to five-year-olds. A well-balanced Foundation Stage curriculum will provide opportunities that address the Early Learning Goals over that two-year period.

● Does your curriculum take into account specific times of the year when certain Areas of Learning will take precedent? September, for example, is a time when children experience change: they will be starting in a new room or beginning at the setting, so it is a crucial time for Personal, social and emotional development. The Early Learning Goal clusters for this are concerned with self-confidence, making relationships and self-care.

General requirements

● The quality of children's learning is categorised under the outcome helping children to 'enjoy and achieve' (one of the four relevant outcomes in *Every Child Matters*) and in the National Standard 3 'Care, learning and play'. Inspectors look for evidence and make judgements as to how well the children are making progress towards the Early Learning Goals.

Tips, ideas and activities

● When putting together your long-term plan, look at the Early Learning Goals together with your staff. Check for any gaps and goals that have not been covered by your setting and imbed these into your future plans.

● Use a spare Foundation Stage document and cross out Early Learning Goals when they are covered. Gaps soon become evident using this visual method.

● Conduct an audit of your resources – a broad and balanced curriculum requires adequate resources for the Early Learning Goals in the six Areas of Learning.

● You should provide activities for physical development throughout the year, as children need to be healthy all year around. There are many physical activities that can be organised in accordance with the relevant Early Learning Goals.

● Weave creative opportunities into all Areas of Learning. Children with limited communication skills can respond to experiences and express themselves with a wide range of materials, imaginative play and movement.

You Can... **Include the Stepping Stones**

The Curriculum guidance for the foundation stage *identifies early developmental stages and describes them as Stepping Stones. They help practitioners to identify the knowledge, skills and understanding that form the Early Learning Goals. They are not age-related but are presented in three parts, grouped according to achievement and coloured yellow, blue and green. Initial development is described in the yellow band, while the green band shows what most five-years-olds could be expected to attain. The Early Learning Goals are described in the grey band.*

Thinking points

● The *Curriculum guidance for the foundation stage* helps practitioners plan to meet the diverse needs of all children. Although the Stepping Stones are presented in a sequence, children's individual progress will be variable and irregular. Children may not 'step' at the same time or in any particular order, but they should all reach the Early Learning Goals by the end of the Foundation Stage.

● The Stepping Stones describe what staff need to know about children's learning. How do you ensure that staff understand the Stepping Stones and use them in their planning?

● Make sure that all the children are given a range of experiences and opportunities to help them develop knowledge, skills and understanding as described in the Stepping Stones.

● Review the Stepping Stones regularly to ensure that they are incorporated into everyday activities.

General requirements

● Inspectors will look for evidence to show that what the children are doing is worthwhile, whether they respond well to experiences and that they are keen to learn. Inspectors will assess the quality of the opportunities provided for the children.

Tips, ideas and activities

● Help staff become familiar with the *Curriculum guidance for the foundation stage*. As a team, examine a Stepping Stone in one Area of Learning and discuss why it is important, how it relates to the Early Learning Goal and how it can be implemented.

● Look at the yellow band for an Area of Learning and discuss the skills, knowledge, understanding and attitudes required to progress through the Stepping Stone. Refer to 'Examples of what children do' (listed next to the Stepping Stones) as these provide good illustrations.

● Discuss how you know a child has made progress in a Stepping Stone. Define the success criteria.

● Consider the section in the guidance 'What does the practitioner need to do?' printed opposite the relevant Stepping Stones, in order to organise and provide appropriate activities.

● Have regular planning meetings to assess the success of activities and monitor child development. Ask how many achieved the Stepping Stone and whether it needs to be revisited.

You Can... **Include the five strands (1)**

There are five strands in the document Every Child Matters. *They are: 1) be healthy, 2) stay safe, 3) enjoy and achieve, 4) make a positive contribution, 5) achieve economic well-being. The Government's ten-year plan for education is centred on these five areas. Ofsted works to these five outcomes and has linked the 14* National Standards *to them in its new documentation. The only exception that settings have to be aware of is that the final outcome differs during inspection. The last strand (achieve economic well-being) has been drawn together under the heading of 'organisation'. This focuses on the management and leadership of the setting.*

Thinking points

● Are all your staff familiar with *Every Child Matters* and the five strands that Ofsted uses for inspection purposes? Do you have enough copies of this document available for everyone?

● How often do you discuss the five strands with your staff? You may find it helpful to use the strands as a focus for your staff noticeboard.

● How often are the strands referred to at staff meetings? Keep putting them on the agenda until they become absorbed by all members of your team.

● Consider management issues – are there areas where improvements can be made? Would further training help? Without good leadership and management there is little possibility of sustainability and economic well-being for the setting.

General requirements

● Inspectors will judge how well you meet the five strands, as well as the requirements laid down in the *National Standards*, how well you provide a suitable curriculum for the Foundation Stage, and how well you implement *Birth to Three Matters* for children in baby and toddler areas.

Tips, ideas and activities

● Display the five strands on the staff noticeboard for all to see.

● Write the five strands on flashcards and keep them with you at all times so that you can refer to them on a daily basis.

● Introduce new staff to *Every Child Matters* and the five strands. Emphasise the importance of being familiar with this document.

● Follow the progress of one child for one day. Then see if staff can place some of the activities completed by the child under the five outcomes for inspection.

● Look at your setting's environment from a child's point of view to see how the strands, such as health and safety, meet the children's needs.

● The setting's team should have identified key staff that focus on areas within each strand, for example, health and safety or special educational needs. How are they performing in their roles? Review their roles and how they could improve.

You Can... **Include the five strands (2)**

It is vital to make sure that your setting meets the requirements for each of the five strands (which are: 1) be healthy, 2) stay safe, 3) enjoy and achieve, 4) make a positive contribution, and 5) achieve economic well-being) outlined in the document Every Child Matters. *For inspection purposes Ofsted uses the overall title of 'organisation' for the final strand. Look at each area in detail as it relates to your setting and take any action as necessary to make sure you match or exceed the* National Standards.

Thinking points

● **Be healthy**: consider how you plan this strand into your curriculum. How often do the children exercise? How healthy are your setting's snacks? Is there a rest area for tired children?

● **Stay safe**: does your curriculum-planning incorporate themes to address safety issues? Do you plan activities that establish what constitutes safe and unsafe behaviour?

● **Enjoy and achieve**: think about how you know that children are enjoying their learning and play. What criteria do you use to recognise the children's achievements?

● **Make a positive contribution**: look at how your setting contributes to the local community and how this can be developed. How does your setting contribute positively to the development of each child in your care?

● **Organisation**: how well organised is your setting? Are your routines and practices organised to fit in with the well-being of the children?

General requirements

● Inspectors will gather evidence relating to the five strands by observing the setting, interacting with the children, talking to the staff and looking at paperwork, policies and photographs. Inspectors will use all these to make a final judgement about the setting's ability to support and deliver the strands effectively.

Tips, ideas and activities

● With your staff, talk about the planning that takes place in your setting: which of the five strands do you cover and how can you cover them all and better?

● Code your curriculum-planning documents as 'long-', 'medium-' and 'short-term' in order to monitor the coverage of the first four strands. The final strand (organisation) is not as relevant for curriculum-planning, but should not be ignored because it does relate to the overall management and leadership of your setting, which in turn will impact on how effective you are at planning a well-balanced curriculum.

● Use the five strands as main headings to work to in your future development plan for the setting. Adapt photocopiable page 62 (you will probably need more than one sheet to cover every area) and complete as appropriate for your setting. Show this to the inspector to demonstrate that you are implementing these strands into the overall structure of the setting.

● Maintain a separate, clearly labelled file for each of the five strands to keep a record of information and evidence that you are working to include these strands in your everyday practice.

You Can... Plan effectively (1): the right impact on the children

In order to plan a well-balanced curriculum for the children in your setting you need to refer to the guidance offered within the Foundation Stage for practitioners for three- to five-year-olds. Birth to Three Matters *offers planning advice for the baby and toddlers age range, but remember that this is a support document and not a curriculum. A well-balanced curriculum offers children a range and variety of activities. Good curriculum-planning should also be well-presented and understood by all of the team.*

Thinking points

● Remember that Ofsted is a regulator and therefore cannot give you direct advice on how to plan.

● How effective are you when you plan your curriculum? What criteria are your planning intentions based on? Are your plans child-centred or do they revolve around what staff would like to implement?

● What action do you take to make changes when your planning is not effective?

● When you plan activities, do you think about how they are timetabled and how this affects the children?

● Do you cram several activities into tight time slots? Effective curriculum-planning means balancing the number and length activities against the needs of children, giving them enough time to absorb and immerse themselves in learning and play, without being rushed.

General requirements

● Inspectors will look out for: activities that are well-planned; sufficient in number and range to avoid boredom and over-stimulation; activities to support the relevant curriculum guidance documents and set at an appropriate level; that staff have a sound knowledge of the Foundation Stage curriculum. They will seek to find the impact of learning on the children.

Tips, ideas and activities

● Any planning documents need to be child-centred, with levels of differentiation in mind. Good curriculum-planning is about balancing and meeting the needs of the children as individuals.

● When planning curriculum activities, ensure that they take into account children's energy cycles. Higher levels of concentration occur once their basic needs, such as rest and food, have been met. Children peak at certain times and get tired too – does your curriculum-planning consider this?

● When planning an effective curriculum, also allow for activities, themes and topics to be revisited in a number of different ways in order to ensure consolidation.

● In the end, the judgement of effective planning lies in the quality of the teaching. Curriculum-planning may appear impressive on paper, but inspectors will want to see how curriculum theory is put into practice, and the impact that this has on the children in your setting.

You Can... Plan effectively (2): the issues of learning, staff and management

Effective curriculum-planning means that children have an interesting and appropriate programme of play on offer to them. Adults must also respond to their needs by taking into account the children's varied interests and all staff should take part in the planning process. Time should be invested in curriculum-planning: this is an aspect of the fifth strand (organisation) that inspectors judge. Curriculum-planning should focus on quality and should take into account your setting's resources.

General requirements

● Inspectors will want to observe how your planning affects the children and see evidence of how you plan your curriculum time, for example, by seeing planning sheets.

● Staff must know the documents related to planning.

● You need to show that you review curriculum-planning regularly and take any relevant action.

● Management should demonstrate that they support staff with curriculum-planning.

Tips, ideas and activities

● Have a focus week on planning – select one children's activity a day and follow it using observations. Discuss with staff what you have learned and consider how your observations can help you plan better.

● Look at other planning examples, perhaps from another setting, for ideas on updating or improving your current system.

● Find out if the Early Years and Childcare Partnership holds any advisory courses on curriculum-planning in your area.

● Make sure your evaluations of curriculum-planning include the cycle of 'plan, do and review', and that this is clear.

● There are time implications for effective planning, but it is important to put time aside to cover all areas of the curriculum.

● Consult with staff and make sure they feel supported by management when it comes to curriculum-planning. Put mentoring schemes in place, if this seems appropriate, and check that any necessary training is taken.

Thinking points

● Effective curriculum-planning means thinking through each individual activity thoroughly. Is this current practice within your setting?

● Are the written plans used in your setting clear and easy to read? Consider revisiting them regularly. Would a parent understand them as well as a new member of staff?

● What evidence can you use to show what effective planning means for your setting? For example, better annotated photographs or observation sheets that include sections on the effect on children?

● Effective curriculum-planning needs to be monitored and evaluated. Is this currently happening, and is this evaluation shared and delegated among all your staff?

● Remember that inspectors see paper-based evidence as secondary: they are more concerned with how you put this planning into practice.

You Can... Address additional needs and inclusion

All children have a right to education, whatever their ability. Early years practitioners need to explain how their provision meets the diverse needs of the children so that most will achieve the Early Learning Goals by the end of the Foundation Stage. Inspectors may ask staff, managers and parents questions regarding equality of access and opportunities for the children. Settings may identify a range of individual needs that require special provision, for example: different ethnic origins, faiths, asylum seekers, refugees, gifted children and those for whom English is an additional language. Some children may be sick or have a disability.

Thinking points

● Are you and all the staff familiar with the requirements and do you work closely with parents?

● Are activities planned to include racial, cultural, social and gender differences?

● Check that all staff are aware of the Code of Practice for SEN. Do they know what to observe, how to record and who to turn to for advice?

● Does current practice in your setting reflect equal opportunity policies?

● Are boys and girls given equal opportunities to use the resources and the activities?

● Do you monitor all staff awareness of the equal opportunity policies and their role in implementing them?

● Make sure that your planning and the setting's environment is adapted for children's differing needs, for example, those who are gifted and more able, those who have English as an additional language or have physical disabilities.

● Do your resources reflect the diverse cultural society?

General requirements

● The *Code of Practice* outlines the legal requirements for children identified with special educational needs (SEN). National Standard 10 also covers additional needs and inclusion.

● Inspectors will ask the SENCO (special educational needs coordinator) for evidence to show how the setting is addressing these issues. Every setting must have a SENCO.

Tips, ideas and activities

● Have a named member of staff responsible for ensuring that appropriate provision is made for those with special educational needs. Ensure staff receive relevant training.

● Use a wide range of teaching strategies, including multi-sensory experiences.

● Audit resources to check that they reflect the diverse cultures within the setting, that they are free from discrimination or stereotyping and are appropriate to the children's physical abilities.

● Adapt the environment and the resources to help children whose abilities are in advance of their communication skills, for example, use signs and symbols and larger text.

● Develop a range of creative activities that reflect the colours, patterns, music and stories of the children's cultural heritage.

● Put time aside to communicate with parents to make sure you take on board their particular concerns for their child. Respond to any worries and explain how the setting plans to meet the children's needs.

You Can... **Balance adult-led and child-initiated activities**

"Growing has to be done by the child, it cannot be done for him by his teacher." (Edmund Holmes, 1912)

Good education is about preparing for real life, and life requires us to make daily choices. Children have to learn how to make their own decisions, become independent and be responsible for their own behaviour. A well-balanced day will include times when adults organise routines and direct learning but also when children are able to exercise choice, initiate their own learning and to manage their own behaviour.

Thinking points

● Provide a range of alternatives for children to make choices and decisions. Are the children familiar with the resources? However, be aware that too much choice and too many alternatives can end up being confusing for children and, therefore, non-productive.

● Make sure the layout of the room allows the children freedom of movement and easy access to resources. It is important to make sure that all the children are able to take part in making decisions and choosing resources.

● Check that staff are available to interact and support children's ideas.

● A high emphasis on always 'getting it right' may make a child afraid to try, so it is vital to stress that it is all right to make mistakes as we always learn from these.

General requirements

● Inspectors will look for evidence that children are given sufficient choices to develop personal independence and autonomy.

● The physical environment in your setting should clearly show that resources are available and accessible, so that children can practise the skills needed to make everyday decisions. Labelling and defined activity zones will support this, and daily plans will provide further evidence.

Tips, ideas and activities

● Plan and resource carefully for independent learning. Be ready to interact, support and carry out the children's ideas.

● Show that the children's choices are respected and valued. Display their work in the setting.

● Introduce self-registration by collecting their name label or photograph and attaching to a list that they can tick every day.

● Label resources clearly or, for younger children, attach photographs of the contents. Encourage the children to select and replace them independently.

● Always have basic mark-making tools available and accessible, such as pencils, crayons, chalk and paper, so that children can record their thoughts and ideas.

● Provide a number of realistic alternatives that support the planned Learning Objectives. For example, for a creative activity have a choice of paint and construction materials available.

● Encourage children to make simple rules, for example, how many children at a time are allowed at the water tray.

You Can... Meet the needs and interests of your children

Capturing children's interest is a key to effective teaching and learning. It is essential to understand their basic physical, emotional and health needs. Children learn through both spontaneous and structured play that feeds the intrinsic feeling of enjoyment and achievement. Meaningful play is an important part of children's experience where they follow their natural curiosity, experiment and discover solutions. They may voluntarily repeat situations or activities in order to gain mastery. Structured play allows the practitioner to plan the development of specific skills.

Thinking points

● Make sure that the learning programme is planned with the children's interests in mind. Is it flexible enough to respond to any unexpected events?

● What signals are the children giving of their current interests?

● Check that your staff can read the children's body language and their signs of involvement and motivation.

● Resources alone do not provide quality learning experiences. Ensure effective interaction from skilled adults, so that resources are used to enhance and develop significant learning experiences.

● Find out the parents' expectations and beliefs about success and failure. Their attitudes may affect how their children approach learning. Emphasise that young children need encouragement and nurturing, and that they have a natural curiosity and a need to explore the wider world.

● Do you bring excitement and wonder to learning situations? Do you make activities stimulating and novel by presenting them in new ways?

General requirements

● The learning environment should be flexible and equipped with sufficient resources to support the six Areas of Learning (as described in the *Curriculum guidance for the foundation stage*) and any special educational needs.

● In addition there should be a wide variety of materials that reflect the children's interests and abilities, and to respect their cultural differences.

Tips, ideas and activities

● Track the children's interests during the day. Where do they play? How long do they sustain interest? What is their level of involvement? Note patterns, likes and dislikes.

● Vary teaching strategies to accommodate different styles of learning, such as: visual, aural, logical, spatial and kinaesthetic.

● Discover innovative ways of incorporating the children's current interests and trends into the learning programme.

● Create a supportive climate where the children know they are valued and respected. Minimise pressure.

● Encourage originality by showing the children there is often more than one way to do something.

● Provide challenges that are achievable and find simple problems to solve by asking, *I wonder why?* or, *How do you think that happened?*

● Young children are still very much involved with the 'I and me', so keep activities relevant to them and their situations.

● Empower children with an 'I can do' mentality. Promote self-esteem by using positive and constructive feedback.

You Can... Support professional development

Recent developments in early years education and childcare have altered the role of practitioners and teachers. The Government has expressed the need for a workforce that is better qualified and the introduction of legislation for National Standards for Day Care and the Foundation Stage curriculum has added increased pressure on staff to develop their knowledge and skills. Better knowledge and skills among staff contribute to a well-balanced curriculum in your setting.

Thinking points

● Consider how you assess staff competencies. Are there gaps in knowledge or skills?

● Do staff have opportunities to attend quality training? Does it help them to deliver the Early Learning Goals in innovative ways?

● Check that staff have the opportunity to explore different approaches in curriculum-planning and teaching.

● One of the changes in the inspection system is that inspectors will look for evidence of the outcomes as described in *Every Child Matters*. Are staff aware of how to provide and promote children's health, how to keep them safe, help them to enjoy their development and learning and how to encourage them to contribute to their own development and that of others?

● Do your professional development objectives cater to the individual needs of staff, while also aiming to benefit the whole setting?

● Make sure that staff know where to get advice, support and funding for training.

General requirements

● The QCA sets the standards of learning and assessment for all children from three to 14 years of age. They also accredit staff qualifications.

● The *National Standards* (1 and 2) require the person in charge to hold suitable qualifications and to ensure that the rest of the staff meet the minimum level of qualifications.

● Inspectors want to see that training is available and relevant to staff, and that your setting is committed to a programme of professional development.

Tips, ideas and activities

● Implement induction programmes for new staff, using buddies or mentors.

● Analyse staff skills, qualifications and interests on a regular basis. Provide training to fill any gaps.

● Encourage staff to develop their areas of special interest and expertise. You might find it helpful to find out from staff individually what their particular interests are and their ideas for development.

● Create a well-structured schedule for staff development based on an annual appraisal.

● Provide a 'professional development file' for all staff, so they can celebrate their achievements and map out their future development. Include dates of appraisals, course certificates and a list of their career targets.

● Ask staff to take one Early Learning Goal and explore the different ways it can be delivered. Exercises such as this will help staff to expand their knowledge, creativity and skills to help deliver a better curriculum.

You Can... **Build links with the curriculum**

Assessment and record-keeping are very important as they track the child's progress and developmental steps through the Foundation Stage. Systems for monitoring children's progress must link to the Stepping Stones outlined in the Curriculum guidance for the foundation stage, *which are there to assist the practitioner. The golden rule of 'plan, do and review' is essential in relation to the Stepping Stones in order for assessment to fit in with curriculum-planning. Parents may also request to see assessments and record-keeping in relation to the curriculum, so samples of these should always be ready for both parents and the inspector.*

Thinking points

● How do you monitor the coverage of the curriculum? Can you identify what areas you have covered and when?

● You may find that some of the Stepping Stones in the Foundation Stage do not fit into planned themes organised by your setting. Have you looked through them and spotted any that could be included in your assessments?

● Are all your staff clear about what to assess and how to record? Are they sure of the assessment criteria and how these link to the curriculum? Could they demonstrate these links to the inspector if asked on the day?

● Is extra training required for staff – especially those new to the setting? All staff should be involved with assessment and record-keeping and be familiar with the system used in your setting.

General requirements

● Inspectors will want to see evidence that assessment and recording is being linked to the curriculum, and that it influences future planned activities.

● Records and assessments should consist of follow-up points that relate to what you will do next to develop the child's skills or knowledge.

Tips, ideas and activities

● Build into your long-term planning, regular assessment of how well the curriculum is being covered by your setting as a whole and by staff. Praise staff for successful coverage and work out solutions for any areas that need more inclusion.

● Explain to parents that your setting is committed to assessing curriculum coverage and links, alongside their children's progress. This helps them feel at ease about the aims of your setting.

● Consider using a display board for parents' evenings to show links between assessment and the curriculum. Take a picture of a child engaged in an activity and next to it show the page from the *Curriculum guidance for the foundation stage* or *Birth to Three Matters*. Add an observation sheet with action points and then show a planning sheet for the next week.

● Collect some samples of the above and keep these in a labelled file to show the inspector on the day of the visit. Build up this file as you work through and finish various projects rather than leaving them until the last minute.

You Can... **Construct a schedule**

Assessment and record-keeping can appear daunting, and constructing a schedule will help you take control and deal with all the necessary tasks. A schedule is a useful tool and enhances the effectiveness of the setting. Setting regular time slots for observations and assessments demonstrates to the inspector that the children are being monitored regularly.

Thinking points

● Constructing a schedule involves deciding on the main focus of assessment, carrying it out, recording the results and then discussing them with relevant colleagues. Is this your current practice? Are there improvements you should make?

● As well as a long-term assessment schedule, do you maintain a weekly planner to decide the frequency and type of assessments or observations that are manageable within that particular week? This will help you to keep on top of the assessment process.

● How often do you allocate time in the schedule to review the overall progress over a specific assessment period?

● Check how you support staff that may be struggling with the assessment and record-keeping schedule.

● Put time aside to discuss with staff the effectiveness of your schedule.

General requirements

● Inspectors will look for a consistent approach to assessment and record-keeping by all staff. They want to see that you have a manageable system in place.

● Children's records should be accessible for inspectors to view. Every child should have educational records as well as health and contact records.

Tips, ideas and activities

● Remember that the schedule should guide staff through the assessments and record-keeping procedure.

● In the schedule, plan in at least one parallel observation a week (where two members of staff observe a child), to help you get different views and perspectives on a particular activity or situation.

● Keep your schedule for assessment and record-keeping with your long-term plan, preferably in the same file. This will show inspectors that development is being managed across various aspects of your setting.

● Hold training sessions for your staff, and ask staff to bring in assessments they have completed so far. Talk about how they are managing them within the scheduled period of time against their overall workload.

● Use photocopiable page 57 as an example of how to carry out an observation.

You Can... Involve parents

Parents are the first educators of their children and they feel proud when their child achieves and concerned when they do not. Assessment and record-keeping in isolation will not give the whole picture of the child. It is important to involve parents and carers in the assessment and record-keeping procedure. A successful assessment result for a child should be celebrated with the child's parents – this can be important for the child's self-esteem. Your setting must give value to the sharing of assessment information, and it must prioritise keeping records of a child's progress in appropriate ways.

Thinking points

● What type of records do you keep to record a child's progress? For example; photographing them at work, keeping a folder or log book of their produced work, tape recordings and a tick list of completed activities are all different methods of recording their progress.

● How often does your setting arrange to meet parents to discuss progress, show them their child's records and discuss any assessment issues?

● Do you encourage feedback from parents regarding any concerns or comments they make regarding their child's progress and assessment? Are your records informative enough for parents?

● Consider what measures are already in place to ensure that action is taken regarding parents' feedback and concerns. Are there improvements to be made?

General requirements

● Inspectors will judge how staff meet the needs of the children, while maintaining records and sharing these with parents. Keep a file of progress records for the inspector to see, and also the type of records you show to parents.

● Inspectors will consider how you record and implement feedback from parents.

Tips Ideas and activities

● Provide a box for parents' suggestions near your setting's doorway or reception area so that parents have the opportunity to comment anonymously, or when a meeting may be inconvenient.

● When a child has completed or achieved something for the first time, write the progress on a postcard to send home with him/her. Leave room for comments and feedback from parents.

● For parents' evening, prepare a board displaying a record of the children's work over a certain period of time or relating to a particular theme.

● Give parents a sheet of short comments about their child's progress. This could be structured to have six boxes representing the six Areas of Learning. Leave space for comments and responses from parents, perhaps using a shared assessment format. Keep these sheets in a file to show inspectors.

● Consider implementing a key-worker system: one person takes responsibility for providing information and regular communication regularly with parents about a group of children they oversee.

You Can... **Keep useful records**

Maintaining useful records is vital to the effectiveness of your setting. All records should be reviewed regularly and kept up to date, especially those records that relate to the requirements of the National Standards for Day Care. Records on a child's health or special needs are also a necessity. Records must be kept in a well-organised filing system. Remember that you will have no warning when an inspector might call, so it is essential that all key staff know where to access the setting's records. Standard 14 relates to the maintenance of documentation, so make sure you are familiar with it.

Thinking points

● Check that staff have an understanding of the definition, purpose and aims of record-keeping. Discuss with them the record-keeping procedures.

● Do you have all the necessary paperwork to show inspectors? Are there any gaps that need to be filled or any irrelevant duplications that need to be discarded? If you know of any, put them in a development plan to show the inspector. Also include your plans to solve these gaps.

● Who monitors and updates your records internally? Do you need to assign this role to someone specific or distribute the responsibility among your team?

● How do you prefer to keep records – on paper or on a computer system? Think about which format would be better for each type of record.

General requirements

● You need to keep comprehensive records to show you are meeting required standards.

● Inspectors will look at records to track the effectiveness of the setting's routines and policies.

● Inspectors will want to know about your methods of record completion and that all staff follow these methods. Use Standard 14 as your guide.

Tips, ideas and activities

● Ask the recipients of your records for feedback regarding their usefulness and their format. Discuss with them if they can be improved in anyway.

● Remember to have a back up for records kept on computer, in case there is a system crash.

● Confidential records should be kept in a safe place and labelled as confidential, whereas others (for instance, information on children and their food allergies) need to be easily accessible for all staff.

● Keeping track records of basic procedures, such as the last fire drill, helps to ensure regularity of your setting's procedures.

● Remember to keep records for the purpose of evidence, for example, any complaints made by staff and parents, or an accident log book.

● Set time aside regularly to update your files and to make sure all necessary forms are complete. This is much better than leaving it until the last moment and being overwhelmed with paperwork.

You Can... **Pass on the right information**

Good practice requires a setting to observe, assess and record children's progress in order to plan appropriate activities and to inform their Foundation Stage Profile. (See page 51.) The Foundation Stage Profile (FSP) is a summary record of a child's attainment at the end of the Foundation Stage. Pre-schools should make available their observations and assessments of children's progress to the receiving Reception teacher if requested. It is essential that children's records are kept safe, secure and confidential. However, their records may need to be shared on 'a need to know' basis with other professionals at times.

Thinking points

● Staff need to feel that their setting is a positive place to be and that they are valued members of a team. Any issues should be aired professionally and these need to be resolved quickly and appropriately. How is this currently achieved?

● Consider what the term 'sustainable' means and think of simple examples to illustrate this in your setting. Ask other staff to do the same.

● Encourage staff to develop, investigate and offer their own solutions to challenges facing them. They are more likely to feel positive about their role and responsibilities, and to be motivated to implement any new undertaking.

● If there appears to be a drop in staff morale, inject some enthusiasm – hold a social evening or provide a small reward.

● You will need to plan ahead to ensure that the positive approaches you put in place are sustained in the future.

General requirements

● Inspectors will look for evidence to show you use your assessments and observations effectively.

● Before any records or assessment information is passed on, you need to be sure that the recipient has the right to know. Parents have the right to access all written information about their child.

● The *Children's Act 2004* and National Standard 14 require certain information to be kept when a child is first admitted to a setting. In addition a record should be kept concerning anything that relates to the child's safety and welfare.

Tips, ideas and activities

● Conduct informal verbal exchanges with parents on arrival and departure at the setting on a daily basis.

● The use of the key-worker system can be helpful. This is where parents can meet a named member of staff who works closely with their child.

● Provide parents with a daily diary or notebook showing activities and any special events undertaken by their child.

● Keep folders with key pieces of work and add comments to show progress and any learning opportunities. Relevant pieces may be sent to the receiving teacher at the school when a child leaves the setting.

● Arrange a meeting for parents to discuss their child's final progress and achievements.

● Keep a dated record of the information passed on to other professionals or settings.

You Can... Develop the Foundation Stage Profile

The statutory Foundation Stage Profile (FSP) follows on from the introduction of the Foundation Stage curriculum. It shows how a child has progressed through the Stepping Stones towards the Early Learning Goals for the six Areas of Learning. It provides an indication of their future learning needs. The information is built up over the years through evidence collected from all the adults who interact with the children. Inspectors will need to see evidence that complies with statutory requirements and that you monitor children's progress.

Thinking points

● Schools and other relevant settings make their assessment and give each child a summary score against 13 scales. Information is passed on to the Year 1 teacher so that planning meets the children's needs. The summary scores for the 13 scales are sent to the LEA.

● The QCA-designed Profile should be easy to understand while providing comprehensive information for parents. The practitioner or headteacher can decide the style of reporting.

● If you decide not to use the QCA optional booklet, how will you collect information and sum up children's progress and make judgements?

● If you are a Reception teacher, you may need to access information on a child's progress from the previous setting.

● Have you considered how you will assess children who have English as an additional language? Do you know where you can access support?

General requirements

● The FSP must be completed in any government-funded setting in which children complete the final term of the Foundation Stage.

● Schools must provide parents with a written report on their children's progress and give them the opportunity to discuss the Profile. If they request a copy of the assessment, the setting must provide it.

Tips, ideas and activities

● Reports should make parents aware of the Early Learning Goals and describe the individual targets their child needs to work towards. Put time aside to discuss with parents how they can help their child's learning.

● Although pre-schools do not have to complete a Foundation Stage Profile, unless they have children reaching the final term of the Foundation Stage before leaving, they do have to have an effective way of maintaining records and observations for each child that shows their progress in the six Areas of Learning.

● Include observations from all staff who interact with the children, for example: dinner staff, the caretaker or volunteers.

● Provide easy ways to record children's achievements or comments, for example, Post-it Notes or a daily diary. Ensure these observations are named and dated by staff. These 'on the spot' observations can then be written into children's individual record books.

You Can... Involve parents and carers with views and feedback

Practitioners must always be aware of the important influence of a child's parents or carers. Developing a good relationship with parents and carers helps a child to feel secure and have a sense of belonging in the setting. It also reassures the parents or carers that you have their child's best interests at heart.

Thinking points

● Check that your setting makes parents feel welcome.

● Think about how you achieve an open and inclusive relationship with parents and remain professional at all times.

● Consider the many varied outside influences that concern parents when you arrange meetings. Can you find ways to accommodate their needs or overcome them?

● Keep the children's records secure and confidential, but accessible to those who need them. Make parents aware of the procedures you have in place to protect their child's privacy.

● Develop channels of communication, both formal and informal, where parents can communicate their feelings, concerns and appreciation of the setting.

● Make sure that any written information given to parents is of high quality, comprehensive and gives correct information.

General requirements

● National Standard 12 requires settings to develop a supportive partnership with parents and carers.

● Inspectors will judge how well a setting informs parents. Good practice depends on parents and practitioners working together. Inspectors will examine how a setting communicates, reports children's progress, involves parents and encourages a two-way exchange of information.

Tips, ideas and activities

● Communicate to parents using a wide variety of methods, being aware of their differing language needs. Use photocopiable page 63 as a template for encouraging feedback.

● When inviting parents to the setting consider the following:
  ● available space for private conversations
  ● timing events to fit in with work, social or cultural needs
  ● mobility or transport issues.

● Show that you value parents' observations and contributions about the child's learning at home. Incorporate the comments into records and portfolios.

● Have the children host a coffee morning for their parents, serving food and drink and showing off their work.

● Set up parents' workshops to disseminate ideas about purposeful play and learning. Include hands-on experiences, such as messy play, making dens and role-play.

● Emphasise shared learning experiences. Show how important it is to get involved and interact with their children.

● Organise ways for parents to volunteer their help and be part of the setting, for example: in the classrooms, as governors or taking part in social events.

You Can... **Liaise with other agencies**

There are times when it is necessary to share certain information about a child with external agencies, such as health visitors, special educational needs advisers, child protection agencies and social services. National Standard 10 requires inspectors to examine children's records and note how well you implement the Code of Practice (2001) for the identification and assessment of special educational needs (SEN). For Standard 12, the inspector considers your partnership with parents and carers.

Thinking points
● Check that all staff know who to refer to, and the procedures to follow, if there is a concern or a sensitive situation.

● Anything that staff see, hear or write should only be shared with parents, managers or appropriate professional support agencies.

● Parents should be informed if you have to pass on information about their child. However, in the case of suspected abuse, this may be done without the parents' consent. The child's needs and welfare must always come first.

● At times you may need to attend a case conference (when all those concerned with the child are brought together). The parents might be invited together with external agencies, such as a family doctor, health visitor, social worker, child protection officer and a psychologist. Make sure that your information is correct. Can you support what you say? (This will be written down.) Everything discussed at a case conference is confidential.

General requirements
● An inspector will look for evidence that staff are aware of the correct procedures for the identification of SEN, behaviour management and child protection, (National Standards 10, 11 and 13).

● National Standard 14 provides a full list of the records required to be kept on the premises.

Tips, ideas and activities
● An accident book and records on the safe administration of medicines should be retained for two years from the last entry to protect you in the event of legal action (National Standard 14).

● Many of your records will cover children's achievement and progress, while others are concerned with personal details, such as names, addresses and contacts. Some of this information may need to be given to the relevant agency when there is an issue about a child.

● Develop a policy on confidentiality and ensure that all staff are aware of procedures when dealing with other agencies. Ensure that they maintain confidentiality when caring for children with special educational needs, emotional and behaviour issues or have child protection concerns.

● Make sure that staff know what to do if there is an accident. It is good practice to tell the parent and explain the situation.

● Display information for parents. This may include where they can access local agencies in the area and where to find health services, financial or emotional support. Always maintain a friendly but professional relationship with parents and refer them to the appropriate agencies to meet their individual needs.

You Can... Foster links with the local community

An early years setting is an important part of any community. It offers an ideal opportunity to bring families together for support or social events and can involve people of all ages – from siblings to grandparents. To a large extent the community links you create will depend on the locality of your setting. Some things will work best in a small rural village, while an inner city offers different opportunities.

Thinking points

● Consider how you inform the community about your setting and how you market your provision. Do you approach places where people congregate, such as libraries, community centres, health centres, supermarkets or post offices?

● Look at what your literature says about your setting. Does it present a professional and positive image?

● Be aware that, whenever you take children out into the community, people will make judgements about their behaviour and the staff.

● Check your current practice. When taking children under five years of age on trips outside the setting (in order to broaden their understanding of the community), it is strongly recommended that you have the parents' consent and conform to the regulation ratios: one adult to two children. It is desirable to have a first aider with you.

● Have you got records (for example, photographs) of activities for the inspector to see?

General requirements

● Inspectors will want to see that your staff ensure that children have experience of the wider world. In the Foundation Stage this includes broadening their understanding of other cultures and beliefs, and developing a sense of place. They need to discover features about their immediate environment and the natural world.

Tips, ideas and activities

● Prepare for any visit outside the setting. Do a risk assessment, consider the health and safety aspects and check out the facilities beforehand.

● Always have a member of staff accompanying any visitor or volunteer who has not been police-checked.

● Arrange inexpensive outings to places, such as: farms, parks, markets, the post office, fire service, and the library.

● Encourage children to meet other children who have a different culture or who have disabilities. Be sensitive and explain there is not just one way of being or living.

● Arrange visits to the children's future primary schools so they get to know the staff and the environment.

● Invite visitors to the setting who have a skill or a talent: artists, musicians, bakers or storytellers.

● Organise open days and fund-raising events and invite local senior citizens to attend.

● Build positive relationships with local firms. They may be able to offer support by providing resources or information.

● Keep in touch with local newspapers by supplying text and photographs of interesting activities or successes.

Preparation for Ofsted starter checklist

Items/issues	✓ or X	Items to be done and date started	Completed – date and signature	Checked by? Located where?
Senior staff briefed and aware of location of key documents or files, inspection day information				
Policies and procedures up to date?				
Staff meeting notes up to date?				
Records of staff inductions				
Records of training booked for staff List of dates, places, courses				
Staff with key responsibilities – aware and training ongoing				
Self-assessment form completed recently?				
Development plan up to date?				
Evidence of parents' views Records of complaints				

Self-evaluation schedule support document

Name of setting:

Date of review:

Reviewed again:

Outcome	Current position – what do you do now and what do you need to do?	Grade corresponding to Ofsted requirement and why	Action and evidence
Helping children to be healthy			
Protecting children from harm and neglect and keeping them safe			
Helping children to enjoy and achieve			
Helping children to make a positive contribution to the provision and community			
Organisation			

Observation and assessment of activities

Adult's name:

Context:

Activity:

Area of Learning:

Cluster:

Learning Objective:

Tick child's box if Learning Objective has been attempted or achieved.
Add comments (see below).

Name	Name	Name	Name	Name
Follow-up activity	Follow-up activity	Follow-up activity	Follow-up activity	Follow-up activity

Some of the things to look for and record in the boxes:
- children's talk and comments
- replies to questions and questions asked
- how well they watch and listen
- concentration levels
- involvement levels
- attitudes (lively, interested, responsive, reluctant, unsure, confident, curious, imaginative and so on)
- suggestions for follow-up work, extension activities or changes to planning.

Work recorded in folders, display, photographs or other _____

Date: Signed:

Leadership and management questionnaire

This is an anonymous questionnaire, so please respond as honestly as possible. Give examples from your own experiences. Your answers will be used in a positive way to inform and improve leadership and management in your setting.

1. Do you think information is shared within the setting regularly, if at all? Do you know what is going on, what is new, what is required? Could information sharing be improved? If so, how?

2. Are policies, aims and objectives of the setting shared with all staff regularly? How is this done? How could this be improved?

3. Are roles and responsibilities clearly defined for staff? How is this done and how could it be improved?

4. Are problems identified quickly and resolved? How is this done and how could it be improved?

5. Are there good opportunities for professional development? What opportunities would you like to see introduced (if any)?

6. Are there opportunities for staff input/feedback within the setting? Could this be improved? How?

7. Is teaching and learning monitored and evaluated regularly? How is this done? How could it be improved?

8. Is your impact on the work of the setting recognised and valued? How is this done? How could it be improved?

Development plan

Name of setting:

Date:

Area for development – links to *Every Child Matters* (such as health, safety and learning)	Methodology How and where	Timings Who and when	Finance/Cost	Monitoring	Quality and achievement and success criteria

Identifying priorities and setting timescales

Complete the grid by writing in your areas for development and assigning priority levels and timescales or completion dates. Once you have identified your main priorities, prepare an action plan.

Area for development	Priority – high, medium, normal	Timescale or completion date

Annual review and professional development

Summarise past performance and establish new goals. SMART Objectives are specific to the person or the job. They can be measured, agreed with the practitioner, realistic and reasonable, and achieved within a time scale.

Name	Job Title
Name of reviewer	Date
Review of past performance and progress to date: Job knowledge Communication skills Member of team Customer/client care Planning/organisation Using initiative Personal contribution	**Strength/area for development**
New objectives: Personal objective 1. 2. 3. Whole Setting objective: 1.	**Success criteria**

Monitoring arrangements		
1.		
2.		
3.		
4.		
Action needed	Monitored by	Target date
Courses mentoring and so on		

Gathering evidence for the five key outcomes

Create a different coloured file for each outcome and, using the suggestions below as a starting point, begin to fill them with appropriate forms of evidence such as photographs, plans and policies. Then, take each outcome in turn and make a list of additional ideas to add to these suggestions. Fasten the individual lists inside the front of each file and add to them as you go along.

Key outcome	Examples of appropriate evidence	National Standards links	Foundation Stage Areas of Learning links
Being healthy	Photographs of children helping to prepare healthy snacks. A sample menu. Photographs of children washing hands before a meal. A weekly planning sheet indicating planned indoor and outdoor physical activities.	7 health 8 food and drink	Physical development.
Staying safe	A copy of the Child Protection Policy. A copy of a risk assessment undertaken before an outing. A recent copy of a safety check on equipment.	4 physical environment 5 equipment 6 safety 13 child protection	
Enjoying and achieving	A copy of the Settling In Policy. Photographs of children engaged in stimulating practical activities. Photographs of children enjoying a range of sensory experiences. Examples of achievement records and planning sheets with clear links between them.	3 care, learning and play	All six Areas of Learning.
Making a positive contribution	A copy of the Behaviour Management Policy. A copy of the Equal Opportunities Policy. Planning sheets demonstrating differentiation to meet needs of individuals. A copy of a parent newsletter inviting participation in activities.	9 equal opportunities 10 special needs 11 behaviour 12 partnership with parents	Personal, social and emotional development. Knowledge and understanding of the world.
Organisation to promote good outcomes for children	Details of how policies and procedures are monitored and reviewed regularly and shared with staff and parents. A list of staff qualifications and recent training attended. Details of staff deployment for a session. A floor plan showing room organisation. A blank record sheet demonstrating how individual progress is monitored.	1 suitable person 2 organisation 14 documentation	

Additional support can be found in the following documents: National Standards for Under Eights Day Care and Childminding, *Department for Education and Skills, 2003;* Curriculum guidance for the foundation stage, *Qualifications and Curriculum Authority, 2000;* Every Child Matters, *Department for Education and Skills, 2003;* Early years:firm foundations, *Ofsted 2005.*

Parents' and carers' questionnaire

The following are suggestions for questions that can be used to gain views and feedback from parents and carers. The sheet can be used in an informal interview or sent home for the parent or carer to complete.

● Are you satisfied with the care your child receives?   YES   NO

Is there anything about the care that you like or dislike?

_____

● Would you be interested in learning about how your child learns by attending a curriculum workshop?
            YES   NO

What Areas of Learning would you be interested in?

_____

● Would you like to be more involved in your child's learning in the setting?   YES   NO

_____

● Are there ways you could support your child's learning at home? For example, by enjoying story books together, cooking, creative play or physical activities.
                                    YES   NO

● What resources would help you do this?

_____

● Are you satisfied with the way the setting shares information with you about your child's care and learning?
            YES   NO
If NO what would you like to be improved?

_____

● Would you like to volunteer a skill or an interest to the children in the setting? For example, oral history: telling how it used to be, cultural: telling how it is, sharing aspects of your home culture.
            YES   NO

● Do you have skills, such as painting, sewing, knitting, cooking, woodwork or pottery? Please describe.

_____

● Would you be interested in taking part in social activities with other parents?   YES   NO

● If you have a complaint about the care provided by the setting, do you know what to do?

    YES   NO

_____

In this series:

You Can:
Create a calm classroom

Noisy classroom?
Stressed children?

Don't worry, You Can: Create a calm classroom offers 50 simply ways to motivate your children and take the stress out of teaching.

ISBN 0-439-96522-5
ISBN 978-0439-96522-4

ISBN 0-439-96523-3
ISBN 978-0439-96523-1

You Can: Survive your early years Ofsted inspection

Don't feel overwhelmed by the onset of an Ofsted inspection - we can help you survive it. This book provides straightforward information and practical advice to support your self-evaluation procedures, whatever the setting, and to achieve a successful Ofsted report.

ISBN 0-439-96534-9
ISBN 978-0439-96534-7

You Can: Use an
interactive whiteboard

This easy-to-follow format provides 50 creative tips on how to get to grips with interactive whiteboards and to use them effectively in the classroom. Whether you are a first-time or experienced user, these books offer a wealth of ideas to make the best use of your interactive whiteboard to teach all the curriculum subjects.

ISBN 0-439-96539-X
ISBN 978-0439-96539-2

ISBN 0-439-96540-3
ISBN 978-0439-96540-8

To find out more, call: 0845 603 9091
or visit our website www.scholastic.co.uk